a message of

Confessions of an Ex-Satanist:
How to protect yourself from evil

Deborah Lipsky

A Message of Hope
Confessions of an Ex-Satanist:
How to Protect Yourself from Evil
Deborah Lipsky

Cover image: iStockphoto.com and Tau Publishing, LLC
Cover and book design: Tau Publishing Design Department

For information regarding permission, write to:
Tau Publishing, LLC
Attention: Permissions Dept.
4727 North 12th Street
Phoenix, AZ 85014

ISBN 978-1-61956-036-9

First Edition August 2012
10 9 8 7 6 5 4 3 2 1

Published and printed in the United States of America by Tau Publishing, LLC
For additional inspirational books visit us at TauPublishing.com

TauPublishing.com

Words of Inspiration

I have read word by word Deborah's book, as she was writing. She would send a copy of each Chapter to me in order to look over and see if it is fully in accordance with Catholic teaching. In the Spiritual Warfare there are areas that are not yet clearly defined by the Church. These areas are often interpreted by individuals according to their own experience, but WITHIN THE FRAMEWORK of authentic Catholic Doctrine.

In her final writing I have not found anything that would be contrary to Catholic Faith. I recommend it as being fit to publish.

Fr. John Bacevicius, OFM
Kennebunk, Maine

Contents

⸻⸻⸻ ✦ ⸺ ✦ ⸺ ✦ ⸻⸻⸻

This book was written for priests, religious, and lay people who take spiritual warfare quite seriously and for those who would like to know what spiritual warfare is all about. It was written by someone who could rightly be called an expert in this field because of her many years as a prisoner in a satanic cult. In this book, Deborah Lipsky uses the experiences of her sordid past to help people who are caught up in an occult lifestyle to escape from the slavery of the satanic movement. In so doing, she continues to suffer the attacks and assaults from the "other side".

Deborah's inspired words of wisdom are also directed to individuals who need to be protected from the "wickedness and snares of the devil". Her last chapter is a practical guide for those who desire to defend themselves from evil influences that plague our culture as a result of atheism and various attacks on human life.

Many priests will be very grateful to Deborah for writing this book, as indeed I am. She writes about things that are not taught in seminaries and are sometimes actually ridiculed. Having worked with Deborah, along with Sr. Francanne, on the production of this book, chapter by chapter, I have come to recognize the awesome respect she has for truth. Because of her autism, it seems that she has a heightened awareness of TRUTH, which has come to her in a number of mystical ways. I shall always appreciate what she has taught me about the spiritual life in general and the spiritual warfare in particular. I hope and pray that you will have a similar experience.

Fr. Joseph M. Doyle, SSJ

Who Should Read This Book?

There is a tendency for many people to skip past the introduction and start right into a book because they feel the introduction isn't that important. This book however, contains vital information on spiritual warfare and is a subject that shouldn't be taken lightly. This book is NOT an auto–biography of my time spent as a Satanist but I will share some valuable insights into how demons work to destroy your relationship with God based on my personal knowledge and experience gained during the years I practiced the dark arts.

As a recovering Satanist I still battle temptations like so many others caught in addictions of all sorts. With the help of the Blessed Mother and all the Holy Angels in this book I will share some of these struggles and strategies to overcome them so that those who are undergoing similar experiences can take comfort in knowing that they are not alone and that no matter how desperate or how dismal your circumstance may be, Heaven is waiting to assist you.

Maybe you aren't afflicted by the occult but know of someone who is. This is a book that will help you better understand what and who you are up against. There will be strategies throughout this book to help you be victorious in your daily battles against the forces of evil that spend every minute of every day plotting against you whether you are a devout Catholic, born again Christian, agnostic, or even an atheist. Demons don't discriminate... if you are human and made in the image of God, trust me they will come after you. The key in winning this battle is to know and understand your enemy.

It is also my sincere desire that this book reaches the person who is struggling now with trying to break free from occult practices because this book is a message of hope; our God is an all loving God ready to forgive even our most grievous faults. All you have to do is ask. If that seems too simple it is because the devil doesn't want you to embrace that simple truth because when you do, God WILL take over and help you through the darkness and back into His light.

It is important to understand that usually (there are always exceptions to any rule) children don't say, "When I grow up I want to be a Satanist," or "There is no God". More times than not unfortunate life circumstances and/or a personal history of abuse starts this downward spiral into the abyss. Children learn morals or a lack there of from their parents. Hatred towards any race, nationality, color, or gender is not imprinted on our soul, but is a learned behavior from those who are role models for children. One day these children will grow up and propagate the same values they learned growing up, whether good or bad. While humanly impossible to break such a cycle of hatred on our own, with

God ALL things are possible! Hating people who hate God for reasons you aren't privy to is only playing into Satan's hands. Remember Jesus died for EVERY sinner, even the murderers, drug dealers, and yes Satanists too. Compassion, mercy, and with prayer is the Heavenly way of viewing such people.

When I was a young child I aspired to be a nun. I was born and raised Catholic. I even went to parochial school for 7th, 8th, 9th, and part of 10th grade. I never wanted to become a Satanist which I did as a late teen and young adult. Sadly, I was born into a generational feud. My father's family was Ukrainian Polish who suffered under the hands of the Nazi's during WWII. My mother's family was Prussian German who suffered and lost everything under the Russians who invaded Germany at the end of the war.

When I was born the generational hatred for each other's nationality placed me as a helpless victim in the crossfire of unresolved hurts and wounds of a war that ended 16 years earlier. I would be the only child; the only lingering reminder of what appeared to one side of my family as an unholy union. Literal curses were slung by my grandmothers on both sides toward me and towards each other. My mom and dad never had a chance under these circumstances. A nasty divorce followed 11 years of bitter strife within our home. On top of that I was autistic but the diagnosis wouldn't come until I was an adult so as a child I was labeled "behaviorally difficult" by the school system that saw my autistic mannerisms as "willful and defiant".

To add insult to injury I grew up in a neighborhood that was rife with racial bigotry especially towards Germans like my mom and me. Because we lived in a home built on cursed ground I witnessed so much demonic activity within our home befitting a Hollywood movie. I saw my first demon when I was only 3 years old and from that point on until my conversion back to Christianity 20 years later, I was physically attacked every night by demons.

Starting in the first grade I was beaten up to and from school by bullies every day. Vile racial slurs were hurled at me. It was common to find swastikas chalked on our driveway with the phrase "Nazi go home". My dad who was a police officer just turned a blind eye towards how my mom and I were being treated by the people in the neighborhood.

When I was six years old, I went picking wildflowers for my mom in the meadow adjacent to the cemetery that was close to our home. A group of teenage boys filled with racial hate who were milling around the tombstones surrounded me and shouted racial obscenities demanding that I drop the flowers and leave. I sensed the sadness that filled my mom's heart. Whenever I brought her some wildflowers it seemed to cheer her up a bit so I wasn't about to be bullied this time. I stood up straight and tall and retorted that I had every right to be there as did they. They stoned me and split my head open and resulted in permanent learning disorders. They were never brought to justice and I never forgot the feeling of being abandoned by our legal system. Unresolved hurts fester over time into ugly wounds without intervention and become like perfume that attracts demons.

The abuse I began to suffer in Catholic junior high school from my peers became so overwhelming I went to the nuns for help. At the time both my mom and dad were "living in sin" with their future spouses. The nuns felt that I would contaminate the other good Catholic families so they rejected my pleas for help. They instructed the other girls to stay away from me.

My mom soon married my stepdad who had an explosive temper and was very abusive towards us. My mom always seemed to justify his violent actions. The nuns whom I so trusted and revered viewed me as a leper ready to infect the entire school because of my parent's sin. I was a child broken by circumstances beyond my control. They also told me that I was unfit material for becoming a nun. Intense abandonment and feelings of hurt gave way to anger and wanting justice and revenge on my part.

At that point all I wanted to do is just scare the nuns with devil stuff. I read books on witchcraft but that didn't sound scary enough so I turned my attention to pure Satanism. No matter for what reason, no matter how justified or valid it seems at the moment, dabbling in the occult will lure your soul into the depths of hell before you even know it.

At that time a wolf in sheep's clothing saw my agony and offered me redemption. I trusted this person as they played upon my feelings of rejection and this person introduced me to the world of Satanism. Brainwashed into believing right was wrong and wrong was right, I stumbled onto a satanic bible and I do know it created a reaction of fear with the nuns. All of a sudden I no longer was powerless. Being feared meant I moved up the food chain and very quickly I studied this book to bring all those who had wronged me to their knees. I may have been an outcast for the rest of my high school days but one thing was certain—my classmates were terrified of me and my lust for this power only grew. I would spend the next 6 years entrenched in the black arts.

I quickly became a "rogue Satanist" meaning I left a coven and chose instead to practice on my own. Even in the black arts, within covens, there are hierarchies and codes of conduct to follow. This made me especially dangerous having no "controls" in place. I specialized in invoking demons and unleashing my fury on anyone who wronged me no matter how small the infraction. I rationalized that forgiveness was a weakness reserved only for victims and not survivors. There was no God of love; otherwise He would have rescued me while I cried out to Him every time I was being abused. God was dead, as Nietzsche said, or so I came to believe. The demons knew my weaknesses and my "sore spots" and preyed on them with their half truths until they became my master and I just their dutiful servant.

The point here is that my turning away from God was truly not my intention. One bad decision quickly led to another because, as this book will reveal, evil spirits are all around us attempting to influence our thoughts. Unless you stay vigilant it isn't a matter of "if", but "when" they will influence your thinking and actions. Let your guard down for one second and they will take advantage of it!

You don't have to be Catholic to gain valuable information from reading this book but it helps. After I left Satanism I joined a religious cult and spent the next 18 years denouncing the Catholic faith and proclaiming that the Blessed Mother was nothing more than a demon in disguise.

It wasn't until 2011 when Our Lady made herself known to me in a very personal way that I saw her love and compassion. Even me, someone who had made it a point to ridicule her in the name of Christianity. She delivered me from my personal demons and the hope she gave back to me is to be shared with all who read this book.

I used to take pleasure bringing born again Christians to their knees if they tried to either "exorcising" my demons or speak to me of Jesus' love. Protestants of all denominations were also "sport" as they quickly buckled under my power when they tried to convert me. However even back then I feared the Catholic priest as I knew, as did my demons, that I was no match for the power that came through him from God. I just knew better than to attempt to take on a priest and the Holy army waiting in the wings to help him.

The Black Mass is a corruption of the Catholic Mass and not some Protestant service. Why do Satanists corrupt the Mass? Because they know the one true church has the Blessed Mother on their side. She will crush the head of Satan!

The Catholic Church wrote a manual for priests to perform exorcisms centuries ago that remains 100% effective today. Hey, even the Hollywood movies depicting demon possessions revolve around a Catholic and not a Protestant exorcism because they work! Do the math: do you want to go into a spiritual battle alone, or do you want the Blessed Mother, the Saints, and all the angels standing by your side?

May this book bring you to a better understanding of just how you can protect yourself against the weapons and hidden strategies that the fallen ones use to destroy your relationship with God.

May God's Love be with you always,
Deborah Lipsky

chapter 1

How Evil Began

In modern culture, the belief that the devil is a real entity is quickly fading away. In our western society, Satan today, is being perceived as nothing more than a joke with his horns, red suit, and pointed tail. Advances in science explain away many old wives tales regarding the world around us. Mental illness which 200 years ago was solely attributed to demonic possession is today explained as chemical imbalances within the brain. Sudden uncontrollable fits of anger while driving that often lead to violent or reckless behavior have recently been classified a disorder known as "road rage". Human beings in their insatiable thirst for knowledge are replacing God with science, psychology and technology.

Every day we are bombarded by evil on television when we see suicide bombers and mass killings, political corruption, violent murders, war, and horrific accidents on the news. There is an increasing trend in reality television to include a lot of gratuitous violence which cause the ratings to soar. More and more television dramas center on a cops and robbers theme. This is a plan of mass brainwashing by Satan to get the people to no longer believe in a devil, but see evil as only a concept or flip side of good. We are rationalizing away demonic influences.

We are so heavily exposed to violence and death on a daily basis through various mediums, that it is desensitizing us to accept violence and mayhem as an unchangeable part of life. This weapon of mass destruction is now being utilized by Satan himself against all of creation. We are caught in a cosmic war of good versus evil. There can be no truce with Satan. There is no choice. Either fight evil or be conquered and enslaved by it.

Before we can become warriors of Christ, it is imperative to know your opponent before engaging them in battle. Gaining as much information as possible about your enemy helps point out weaknesses that can be used against them. It is no different in spiritual warfare. Our best source of information on who Satan is and where he came from comes from both the Old and New Testaments. Let's start with how evil began by looking into the Old Testament.

Both Isaiah and Ezekiel in their prophecy against the king of Tyre and the king of Babylon are actually also talking about Satan. In Ezekiel 28 starting with verse 12 we read,

"Son of man, take up a lamentation upon the king of Tyrus and say to him, thus says the Lord God; you sealed up the sum of wisdom, and you were perfect in beauty. You have been in Eden, the garden of God; every precious stone was your covering, sardius, topaz, and the diamond, beryl, onyx, and jasper, sapphire, emerald, carbuncle and gold; the workmanship of your timbrels and your pipes were prepared in you on the day you were created. You are the anointed Cherub that covers; I have set you so: you were upon the holy mountain of God; you walked up and down amidst the stones of fire. You were perfect in your ways from the day you were created, until iniquity was found in you. By the multitude of your merchandise, they have filled you with violence, and you sinned: therefore I will cast you as profane out of the mountain of God: and I will destroy you, oh covering cherub, from the midst of the stones of fire. Your heart was lifted up because of your beauty; you have corrupted your wisdom by way of your brightness: I will cast you to the ground; I will lay you before kings, so that they may behold you." (Ezekiel 28:12–17, revised KJV)

In the New Living Translation bible verse 14 reads, "I ordained and anointed you as the mighty angelic guardian. You had access to the holy mountain of God and walked among the stones of fire." In this verse we see that this Being was assigned the duty of guardian. A guardian is someone who guards, protects, or preserves.

While Ezekiel is prophesying about an earthly king, we can deduce that he is also talking about Satan. Why? First off there is no historical evidence that the king of Tyre fit this description. During Ezekiel's life there was a prince of Tyre but he was overthrown. Clearly in verses 12–17 we see that in no way can this pertain to a mortal king. In verse 12 he was as brilliant and perfect as the precious stones that covered him. Verse 13 places this "king" in Eden, and we know that only Adam, Eve, God, and the serpent Satan were there. Verse 14 calls him the anointed cherub, and in verse 17 he is cast down to earth. Verse 14 says "You are the anointed cherub" and not 'an' anointed cherub conveying a rank or title that sets him above other angels.

The prophet Isaiah adds more detail as to what was the cause of this expulsion from heaven. In Isaiah 14 starting with verse 12 we read, "How you have fallen from heaven, Lucifer [morning star], son of the dawn! You have been cast down to earth, you who once laid low the nations. You said in your heart, I will ascend to the heavens; I will raise my throne above the stars of God; I will sit enthroned on the mount of the assembly on the utmost heights of Mount Zaphon. I will ascend above the tops of the clouds; I will make myself like the most high. Yet down to the nether world you go to the recesses of the pit. (Isaiah 14:12–18, NIV)

So in Isaiah 14 we are given a clear picture that pride filled Lucifer's (also known as the morning star) heart. 'I will ascend to the heavens", "I will raise my throne", "I will sit enthroned", "I will ascend above the tops of clouds", and "I will make myself like the most high". Pride never travels alone. It brings along friends called jealousy, sense of entitlement, and lust. Between Ezekiel and Isaiah we have this picture of a powerful angel who was created by God and set in a position of authority here on earth. This perfect being walked the holy mountain of God and appears to be gifted with music, "The workmanship of your timbrels and your pipes were prepared in you on the day you were created" (Ezekiel 28:13 KJV). Lucifer was in the Garden of Eden apparently before Adam and Eve were created. Somewhere along the line Lucifer began to feel like he was entitled to more than God gave him. "I will raise my throne" (Ez. 28:14) indicates that he was in a position of rulership over the earth with a likelihood of angels underneath his authority. Lucifer became jealous of God's plan to create mankind and place them on earth. Lucifer decides to go up to heaven and overthrow God.

In Revelation chapter 12:7–9 we read of the battle that ensued in heaven. "And there was a war in heaven; Michael and his angels fought against the dragon, and the dragon and his angels fought back, but he wasn't strong enough and they lost their place in heaven. The great dragon, was hurled down, that ancient serpent, called the Devil or Satan, who leads the whole world astray. He was hurled to the earth, and his angels with him" (Revelation 12:7–9, NIV).

Satan was cast out of heaven with one third of the angels who now were fallen angels or demons. "His tail drew a third of the stars of heaven and threw them to the earth" (Revelation 12:4, NIV).

Jesus even speaks of this incident in Luke 10:18 (KJV), "And He [Jesus] said unto them [his apostles], I beheld Satan as lightning fall from heaven."

So what we have here is a created angel who was given authority by God to watch over and protect the earth. This Lucifer had angels under him here on earth. Somewhere along the line he decides that he is entitled to more and wants to be higher than God. As this jealousy gains momentum his thoughts turn to overthrowing God and a war breaks out in heaven. Lucifer gets his butt kicked by Michael the archangel and is now cast not into hell but to the earth along with "his" angels which are now demons. Lucifer's name becomes Satan which means "the accuser" in Greek. Revelation 12 goes on to describe, "For the accuser of our brothers who accuses them before our God day and night has been hurled down... But woe to the earth and the sea because the devil has gone down to you! He is filled with fury because he knows his time is short" (Revelation 12:10, 12 NIV). Satan's mission: destroy mankind.

Satan is in the Garden of Eden when Adam and Eve were created. His jealousy and hate towards God is so great he decides to go after what God created in his image as revenge for being cast out of heaven. Imagine being in the Garden of Eden and seeing these newly created beings wandering around as a reminder of God Himself. Since Satan was cast back to the earth, every time he saw Adam and Eve I am sure it fueled his hate. He devises a brilliant plan to thwart God's new creation by using half truths and all out lies to deceive the man and woman. In Genesis 3:1 we read, "Now the serpent was craftier than any of the wild animals the Lord God made. He said to the woman, did God really say, you must not eat from ANY of the tree in the garden?" (NIV) Note Satan very subtly uses doubt and a half truth by asking if God said all trees were off limits. God in Genesis 2:16–17 gives Adam this command, "You are free to eat from any tree in the garden; but you must not eat from the tree of knowledge of good and evil, for when you eat of it you will surely die" (Genesis 2:16–17, NIV).

God said to Adam only 1 tree was off limits but Satan twists God's warning around slightly by questioning what God really said. In a sense he asked Eve, "Did God really mean you can't eat any fruit from any tree?" He creates doubt and second guessing on the part of Eve on God's instruction. Note Eve's reply, "We may eat fruit from the trees in the garden; but God did say, you must not eat fruit from the tree in the middle of the garden, and you MUST NOT TOUCH IT, or you will die" (Genesis 3:2–3, NIV). Eve adds the admonition to not even touch it despite the fact God never said that. That little bit of dishonesty wets Satan's whistle. He knew his plan was working. He put out a question that was a half truth and she replies back in kind with a half truth. As they say today, "he baited the hook and she was nibbling". Satan wants to "reel her in" so he continues on, "You will not surely die, the serpent said to the woman, for God knows that when you eat of it your eyes will be opened and you will be like

God knowing good and evil" (Genesis 3:4–5, NIV). He calls God a liar! Satan then plants the seed of doubt, pride, and forbidden desire in Eve.

That was just the start of Satan's mission to destroy mankind. The Old Testament is littered with his casualties just to name a few: the murder of Abel (Genesis 4:8), pharaoh's order to kill all first born males when Moses was born (Exodus 1:15), the children of Israel worshipping a golden calf while Moses was getting the ten commandments (Exodus 32:1–6), King David's order to murder Uriah because David got his wife Bathsheba pregnant (2 Samuel 11), Job's persecution by Satan (Job chapter 2), and King Herod's massacre of all male children under the age of two (Matthew 2:16–18).

It is important for you to realize that Lucifer the Devil now known as Satan was created before Adam. As an angel he was made much more superior than mortal man. He has had thousands of years to study our behaviors; our weaknesses and innermost fleshly desires here on earth! All that time spent gaining knowledge and perfecting his evil ways to separate us from the love of God. Being cast out of heaven has made him set his sights on revenge. His apparent victory of making sure Jesus was crucified back fired on him big time by Christ's resurrection , only fueling his hatred towards us even more. He has an agenda. To destroy you and me would be the greatest and most personalized way of attempting to get back at God for his being thrown out of heaven and losing his role of guardian or protector of the earth.

Satan was allowed to come before God on occasion to accuse the faithful of evil and all sorts of lies. In Zechariah and Job we see Satan coming before the throne of God from time to time during man's history. Satan is accusing Joshua the high priest of all sorts of lies before God. Zechariah in a vision from God says, "Then he showed me Joshua the high priest standing before the angel of the Lord and Satan standing at his right side to accuse him. The Lord said to Satan, the Lord rebuke you Satan! The Lord who has chosen Jerusalem rebukes you." (Zechariah 3:1–2, NIV).

In Job, Satan once again is before the throne of God and this time we are shown what Satan does and where he goes. "One day the angels came to present themselves before the Lord and Satan also came with them. The Lord said to Satan, where have you come from? Satan answered the Lord, "from roaming through the earth and going back and forth in it" (Job 1:6–7, NIV).

Here we have the devil who says that he has been roaming the earth studying all that is happening in the world. That means taking note of man's behaviors and actions. Clearly Satan is living with us right here on earth today!! No place on earth is off limits to him.

Note that God in the next line informs Satan that there is one man in all the earth who resists evil and remains faithful to God. "Then the Lord said to Satan, Have you considered my servant Job? There is no one on earth like him; he is blameless and upright, a man who fears God and shuns evil" (verse 8). This must of have really infuriated Satan and caused his jealousy to take over because Satan rationalizes away Job's faithfulness to God. "Does Job fear God for nothing? Satan replied. Have you not put a hedge around him and his household and everything he has? You have blessed the work of his hands, so that his flocks and herds spread throughout the land. But stretch out your hand and strike everything he has and he will surely curse you to your face" (Verse 9–11). Wow, Satan basically whines that Job never had to work for anything, that everything was handed to him on a silver platter by God. Satan is sulking! He is so jealous of Job's faithfulness that he challenges God. He basically says, "Give him to me for a while and watch me break him so that he will come to hate you!" God replies, "Very well then everything he has is in your hands but on the man himself do not lay a finger. Then Satan went out from the Lord's presence" (Verse 12). God allowed this testing to prove Satan wrong.

Read the story of Job and you will be given great insight into some of the weapons Satan uses against Job and all of us today. If Satan is allowed before the throne of God, then he freely can enter into any church today. No physical place here on earth is truly safe from him. If he was in the Garden of Eden and before the throne of God after his fall, there is no place you can hide from him. In 1st Peter we are warned, "Be sober, be vigilant; because your adversary the devil, as a roaring lion walks about, seeking whom he may devour" (1st Peter 5:8, Revised KJV). Here is a clear warning that Satan is on the prowl wanting to devour those who aren't on guard against spiritual attacks by the Devil and his cohorts.

Jesus himself was under attack by Satan on numerous occasions. Before He began His ministry Jesus engaged in an epic battle with Satan who wanted to destroy the savior of the world. Jesus was the redeemer of mankind bridging the gap between man and God. Through His death we humans would be offered salvation and reign with him in His future kingdom. We are destined to do what Satan gave up and that really makes Satan angry! Jesus readies himself for this battle through prayer and fasting. Chapter 4 of the gospel of Matthew gives a blow by blow account of how Jesus battles Satan and comes out the winner right at the start of His ministry. "Then Jesus was led by the Spirit into the desert to be tempted by the devil. After fasting 40 days and nights, he was hungry. The tempter came to him and said, if you are the Son of God, tell these stones to become bread. He [Jesus] answered, it is written that man doesn't live by bread alone, but on every word that comes from the mouth of God" (Matthew 4:1–4, NIV).

Twice more Satan tries to tempt Jesus, each time getting more brazen and grandiose in his temptations. Satan offers Jesus everything this entire world has to offer physically. All Jesus has to do is to kneel before him, renounce God and worship Satan. The Devil is challenging authority and attempting to justify defiance with half truths in order to deceive Jesus by quoting scripture. Verse 5 and 6 say, "If you are the Son of God he said, throw yourself down for it is written: they [angels] will lift you up in their hands so that you will not strike your foot against a stone". Satan was actually quoting scripture! Psalm 91 verses 11 and 12 read, " He will command his angels concerning you, to guard you in all your ways; they will lift you up in their hands so that you will not strike your foot against a stone" (NIV). Here is a blatant example of how Satan can twist scripture in attempt to confuse and lead us astray. In verse 10 Jesus replies, "Get away Satan!"

My point here is that if the Devil went all out trying to tempt the Son of God to get him to fall, how much more will he come after you and me? Satan is filled with hate against God for being thrown out of heaven. He is equally consumed by hate over the fact that Jesus became our perfect sacrifice; atonement for our sins so we could have a personal relationship with God. Every human being that ever lived and is alive now is a constant reminder to Satan that we are made in God's image. If Satan hates God, he hates all the more those made in His likeness which means you and me. In Satan's mind the only thing worse than that is the fact that Jesus plans on returning and banishing him and his demons to the abyss. That thought has Satan so enraged that he has taken off his boxing gloves and he is pulling out every dirty punch he can conceive of to destroy us in mind, body, and soul. He is a very dangerous entity with supernatural powers that we don't have. He has many demons and "legions" at his command (Matthew 8:28, Mark 5:1) who are eager to seek the ruin of our souls. As a spirit being he can travel anywhere through metaphysical mediums we as carbon based creations can't. Ephesians 2:2 refers to Satan as, "the mighty prince of the power of the air". In the bible Satan takes mortal form only three times: as a serpent in the Garden of Eden, in Judas Iscariot, and finally as the antichrist or "man of sin will be revealed, the son of perdition" (2 Thessalonians 2:3, KJV). The rest of the time he is in spirit form that can move freely even through the air.

If this realization overwhelms you, don't worry. In the end Satan will be defeated once and for all by Jesus. "And the devil that deceived them was cast into the lake of fire and brimstone, where the beast and the false prophet are, and shall be tormented day and night forever and ever" (Revelation 20:10, KJV). Until then though, you and I must either become spiritual warriors or helpless captives of the Evil One. The choice is yours. Each chapter will contain invaluable insights into how demons work from someone who was entrenched in the black arts. Do not feel you are alone in this battle. We have the Blessed Mother, the Holy Angels, and Saints by our side.

chapter 2

The Confession of an Ex-Satanist

Iwas born with a special gift from God that allows me to be highly attuned to the spirit world. I come from a long line of women on my mom's side that had this ability. At an early age my mom introduced me to the supernatural world through her relating ghostly encounters from her side of the family. They were mainly dark tales of malicious encounters with the occasional recall of a protective entity acting as a guardian angel. My grandmother had this second sight too. I knew her only a short time before she died when I was in my early teens. She was an extremely religious devout Catholic haunted or hunted by less than benevolent spirits all her life.

I remember every time we visited her in Germany, our visit was plagued by evil supernatural happenings. She spent a lot of time in prayer which I feel helped her tremendously accept the fact she was constantly plagued by such menacing paranormal activity. Back at home I had the ability to actually see demonic presences that invaded my bedroom. Often they would slap or grab me during the night to the point that I learned to sleep in a certain position so as to fend off their attacks. I was very afraid but my pleas were seen as just a childhood "bogeyman" phase by my parents. My mom did however encourage me to embrace this 'second sight' and not be afraid of what she thought might just be restless ghosts.

As a young child I turned to the Blessed Mother and the angels for protection from the unholy night visitors. I used to talk to Our Lady all the time especially during the times I was being victimized by those around me. No matter how badly I got beat up, I felt her consoling presence. It is hard to imagine that as a teenager I would go from loving to hating her. I believe one of the reasons I ended up hating the Blessed Mother so much was because the nuns who turned me away in my time of need wore habits with the veils. To me nuns looked very similar to Our Lady and I thought since they sort of looked like her, they would have the same level of love and compassion as she did. Of course they were human with human weaknesses, but I naively thought they were above that. It took a lot of courage to ask for help. To be told I deserved the abuse I was suffering was soul crushing. There are no words that accurately describe the level of hurt and rejection one feels upon hearing this, especially from those who committed their lives serving God.

Attracted by my anger, demons began to hover around me. They whispered lies in my ear trying to make a mountain out of a mole hill. The more they over dramatized the situation regarding the nuns, the more it suppressed reason allowing unbridled pent up negative emotion to burst forth and cloud my judgment. Unchecked anger is easily molded into revenge by the fallen ones. Other serious childhood issues that caused so much pain provided a breeding ground of negativity that demons capitalized on and used to convince me that the Catholic Church was nothing more than a puppet religion with the Pope as its puppet master. By this point my mind was so polluted by their influence that I turned to the occult as a way to seek revenge against the nuns who turned me away.

I started out in witchcraft. I found books in the library (back before the PC and internet were invented) on witchcraft and studied black magic. I would scare the nuns with childish pranks such as proudly displaying my large black book on witchcraft also called 'the book of shadows', and drawing pentagrams on all my homework and tests. On numerous occasions when I received after school detention, I would intimidate the nuns in charge of my detention by telling them that my god was more powerful than theirs. If they were foolish enough to enter into a debate over the issue, I would summon a demon with a chant. Then I would flash an arrogant smile as some minor demonic manifestation occurred like chalk flying off the chalk board.

I walked around school with an air of superiority and threaten to cast a spell on anyone, including my teachers, who treated me badly. You have to understand that I was the victim of abuse and showed outward signs of that which made me the brunt of ridicule by my classmates. Their constant harassment in both words and actions along with the high school's refusal to intervene and stop the bullying pushed me to the brink.

With my home life in turmoil due to a nasty divorce, and school a hellish nightmare, I felt alone and vulnerable. Every day in parochial school I was mercilessly bullied, harassed, and tormented by my classmates. At home all the constant fighting and yelling between my parents created a sharp rise in evil paranormal activity within our house that intrigued me due to my interest in black magic. I wanted to harness this energy so that I could direct it towards those who wronged me, namely the kids who bullied me and the nuns at school. I studied my craft at the nearby cemetery so as to connect with grief and death. This helps opening portals to the spirit world.

Growing up in the town adjacent to Salem Massachusetts where the infamous witch trials occurred also added to the mystique of witchcraft. There were local legends regarding witches including the 300 year old tree at the end of our property that supposedly was the sight of a witches' hanging. Admittedly it had a creepy sense about it. Whenever I walked past it I could sense an evil presence lurking within its branches. At this point I wanted to make contact with it just to see if I could actually communicate with a disembodied entity. While I never achieved my goal of speaking to this presence, I did actually see its ghoulish silhouette often hanging from a ghostly noose during a full moon.

Also about this time I was befriended by someone who convinced me that I deserved a better lot in life than I had been given by God. God, according to him, was nothing more than a lame duck deity who had neither power nor desire to intervene in man's affairs. If God were real he would have rescued me from my childhood hell is what this man kept drilling into my head. After a while it made sense and I came to believe that God was a cruel task master haphazardly tossing out crumbs of reward only in a flight of fancy to a select few. This man courted my deepest unfulfilled desire to be accepted and valued with promises of power and prestige. He cleverly placed ideas in my head on how to terrify those that were mean to me. All I had to do was to embrace the forces of darkness and call upon these entities to do my bidding. He assured me as a third degree (high priest) Satanist that if I worshipped Satan instead of God, I would be feared by all those who had tormented or wronged me. I would have the ability to conjure up demons and get them to do my bidding. Never again would I have to be a helpless victim of circumstance. Being young, impressionable, desperate for acceptance, and victimized by abuse, I was seduced by thoughts of how power and control over others would empower me. The satanic motto of, "If a man smite thee on the cheek, smash him on the other!" offered a way (albeit perverted one) in which I could defend myself from my abusers.

The Satanist realizes that man is solely responsible for everything, and doesn't mislead himself into thinking someone cares. It mocked the very church institution that turned me away in my time of need. One of the nine satanic principles states that Satan is the Catholic Church's best friend she ever had, for Satan has kept it in business all these centuries.

Although I embraced Satanism as my new faith I couldn't deal with being in a coven. The Black Mass which was a complete mockery of the Catholic Mass still turned my stomach for reasons I couldn't define. I couldn't embrace this ceremonial ritual so I abandoned the notion of joining a coven and went "rogue". Rogue means I practiced black magic and invoked demons without any coven affiliation. I no longer was a neophyte (initiate) but now bestowed upon myself the rank of high priestess that could make up the rules as I went along. I devoted all my energies into channeling demonic forces. That means allowing demons to use my body to communicate. In a sense it is a temporary form of possession but more on this subject in a later chapter. I also NEVER harmed nor sacrificed any animal during this time. It is a misconception by the general public that Satanists are big into animal sacrifices. As we will see in a later chapter, demons aren't interested in animal blood sacrifices. Unfortunately, small bands of rogue satanic wanna be's do mutilate animals during a ritual, but they are the uneducated in what real Satanism entails.

Pride filled my heart. By the time the euphoric high of commanding respect out of people because they feared me wore off, I had already given my free will over to the demonic. As time went on my sense of empowerment turned into enslavement as the demons I invoked began to torment me nightly. They turned on me due to a universal law in black magic I was unaware of. That law states that whatever demon you conjure up to harm someone else can and will come back to you. Also, pacts made with demons center around seven years of the earthly desires in exchange for your soul.

It was in the last part of my sixth year that the demon I made a pact with decided to prematurely collect his part of the deal. After all they don't play fair. Things in my room would be flung around by unseen hands. My dog that slept with me became so terrified of being in my room that one night she clawed her way through a wood door just to escape. They would create horrific nightmares and force me to wake up so many times each night that I became sleep deprived. Demons would materialize into grotesque creatures of the undead (uglier than decaying zombies) at the foot of the bed and brainwash into me that I had nothing to live for and that my soul was theirs now.

Over a period of just a few months they would brainwash me into thinking that I was so hopeless and beyond redemption because God had never loved me because I was unlovable. I had such hopelessness aggravated by my guilt of having abandoned God and the Blessed Mother. Falsely the demons convinced me that it was useless to beg God for mercy and forgiveness.

I wanted out of Satanism at this point. I finally realized I made a mistake. The more I dwelled on the idea to get on my knees and ask for God's forgiveness, the more intense and ferocious the nightly intrusive demonic attacks became. Having become so worn down physically and emotionally, I lost all resolve to stay trapped in a war I could no longer fight. Demons will continue tormenting their subjects up until the last breath so as to avoid a death bed confession. They are well aware of the forgiveness that is available right up to the last moment. They don't want you to become the "big fish that got away". I resigned myself to believing that God would refuse to forgive me for what I had become and done. I surrendered to my tormentors the most precious possession I possessed; my soul.

Having just relinquished my soul to the devil out of desperation, I felt overwhelming hopelessness and a desire to end my life. In my tortured mind, my soul was already dead and decaying. Every breath was a painful reminder of the hell I was living. As a Satanist I viewed those tortured souls who attempted suicide but failed as attention seeking cowardly vermin. I even praised those who succeeded on their first attempt as heroes. I didn't tell anyone about my intent because I didn't want anyone to stop me. I had abandoned all hope. There was no help hotline I could call that dealt with the demonic. My situation had become so grave that human intervention was no longer possible. Like a mortally wounded deer I was defenseless against the pack of wolves that took me down. As the demons closed in for the kill, I had a lone thought of true heartfelt remorse. It was quickly crowded out by the thoughts of demons.

I went to bed on the night of January 14, 1983 resigned into jumping to my death off the railroad bridge at the edge of town the following morning. An angel so powerful that my demonic tormentors (who invaded this dream) cowered away from his radiance appeared to me in a dream. He told me that I was still in God's kingdom. I was told it wasn't my time to die as I had work to do for God yet in this lifetime. He told me that God had felt my heartfelt remorse and desire to beg for His forgiveness and mercy. God also knew I was too deeply obstructed by a legion of demons to be able to remember I had free will to choose God or Satan. Our loving God understood how one bad decision after another stemming from the abuse I endured as a child cascaded into the inescapable hell I created for myself. This angel formed a circle of protection around me that kept the demons out of my reach.

What transpired next is engraved into my memory so that it is still as vivid and real today as it was that night. In an act of pure love and mercy, with the demons unable to access my reasoning abilities, I was asked to choose between God and Satan. The decision would solely be mine and not manipulated by the demons. In that moment I had such clarity that I hadn't had in years. For the first time in my life I felt loved unconditionally by God. In that moment I chose God. In a final admonition I was told that my battle with breaking the hold the demons had over me would be very difficult throughout my life, but all I had to do is ask for help and heaven would come to my aid. Whether this encounter was just a dream or a divine revelation is unimportant. What is important is what I did as a result of it. What mattered was that the severe unrelenting nightly demonic attacks stopped as a result of this heavenly encounter.

The next thing I knew it was morning and I awoke refreshed full of hope and not feeling suffocated by the hopelessness that had crippled my life. In true Saul to Paul conversion, from that moment on I turned my life around forever abandoning my satanic allegiance. The first act of my conversion was running to the confessional the following Saturday before Mass. I was filled with eagerness to purge my soul of all the evil sins I committed over the past six years. Unfortunately, the priest of this parish oversaw the parochial school I had once attended and witnessed my descent into Satanism while I was a student there. He was the priest in the confessional I attempted to confess my sins to. He erroneously concluded that I was blaspheming the church with a mock confession. To him I was just pulling a perverted satanic prank over on him.

I stepped out of the confessional shell shocked by his verbal wrath and refusal to absolve me of my sins. Completely blindsided by this encounter, I froze in my tracks and couldn't take a step in any direction. It felt like someone thrust a knife in my back. I gazed at the statue of Our Lady perched on a pedestal next to the confessional. While I waited for the priest to exit the confessional, I pleaded with the Blessed Mother to intervene in helping the priest understand my sincerity. When he did come out I tried desperately to explain to him how my dream of the angel was responsible for my miraculously instant conversion back to Christianity. With a spirit of total disbelief he said modern day miracles like mine don't exist and aren't real. He asked me to leave.

Familiar intense feelings of extreme hurt began to well up deep inside me. For the second time in my life I desperately needed the church's help. For a second time in my life my plea for help would be rejected by the very institution I placed all hope in. To be thrown out of church added salt to an already gaping wound. All the euphoria I had felt over my miraculous liberation completely evaporated in an instant. My unconfessed sins gave birth to familiar old feelings of anger and revenge. I lashed out at the priest and told him that he and his church could go to hell. As I walked past the statue of Our Lady I told her I hated her because she refused to intervene. My trust in the Catholic Church at that moment shattered into a million little pieces. Why would God offer me redemption from my satanic past and then deny forgiveness from His church?

Demons will use others to knock you off balance just to get you to question and doubt your faith. In my case the priest at that moment was vulnerable to demonic thought tampering. Seizing on the opportunity, they used him as the vehicle of their retaliation towards me. They used him to try to instill a sense of doubt that the angel who came to me in the night wasn't real and that I was still enslaved by Satanism.

On my way home from being kicked out of church I stopped at the donut shop to have a coffee and mull over what had just happened. I sat at the counter next to a young man my age. He was overly happy and cheery in his verbal exchanges with the customers standing in line to get coffee to go. I couldn't help but notice the silver belt buckle he wore that was as big as a hubcap emblazoned with "Jesus saves!" in big, bold, gold lettering. As I stared into my coffee cup trying to make sense of where I was to go from there, this young man turned to me and with a big smile told me that Jesus loved me. I snapped back by calling him a Jesus freak. He replied by saying that he would rather be a freak for Jesus then be a friend of Satan. I retorted by saying he hadn't a clue what it meant to be a friend of Satan. Then I told him about my satanic past, the angel dream, and the rejection by the priest to absolve me of my sins. He listened patiently, but more importantly, he believed my story. He stood up and gave me the warmest hug I have had ever received and said, "Welcome sister to the body of Christ." With open arms he showered me with acceptance and compassion; the compassion that was denied to me in the confessional.

Over multiple cups of coffee we talked for hours that night. He gave persuasive arguments on how the Catholic Church was not the way to get to heaven. He convinced me that the priestly rejection I received was in fact a message from God that the Catholic road led straight to hell. This appealed to the sense of overwhelming abandonment I felt from the church. I accepted and attended his invites to various revival meetings and Christian young adult activities. How ironic to be among the born again Christian movement as a believer when they were the ones I used to torment for fun while still a Satanist. Still, I wasn't comfortable with their ridiculous outlook that as believers all they had to do was invoke Jesus' name to make the devil flee from their lives. As a former Satanist my interactions with demons gave me valuable insights into their nature and behavior. They weren't simplistic entities easily cast off by just speaking the name of Jesus. It wasn't long before I became disillusioned with the born again movement and left searching for God elsewhere.

Over the next couple of months I tried attending services of various Protestant denominations searching for God to no avail. One day I stumbled upon free copies of a religious magazine at a burger joint while waiting for my order. The articles spoke about how Satan was actively working against God in this world and in our lives. The disillusionment we felt with today's churches was God's wake up call to become one of the select few he is calling now to become part of the one only true church here on earth; the World Wide Church of God led by Herbert W. Armstrong, God's modern day apostle and prophet.

He made it his crusade to attack, discredit, and destroy the Catholic Church in his teachings. The Roman Catholic Church was the great counterfeit religion spawned by Satan himself. We were banned from wearing, displaying, or owning crucifixes, crosses, angels, or depictions of Jesus. His doctrines stripped away any and all belief in the Blessed Mother, angels, and all the Saints leaving me inadequately prepared to battle the demonic realm later on in my life.

Mr. Armstrong's teachings provided supposedly biblically proven facts as to why the Catholic Church was the great counterfeit religion devised by Satan to deceive the masses. My unresolved hurt caused by that failed confessional incident turned into seemingly justifiable and righteous hatred against the Catholic Church. I would spend eighteen years as a baptized member of this cult. We were ordered to leave our friends and family if they did not accept our faith. Marriage outside of the church was forbidden and we were only allowed to marry baptized members from within.

Our concept of Jesus was so different than mainstream Christianity. Accepting Jesus into your heart, having a personalized relationship with him, or seeing him as a friend was unacceptable. The trinity also was forbidden and seen as strictly a pagan concept.

I was baptized in October of 1986 and then married in September of 1987 to my current husband. I concluded that this was God's church because the demonic attacks that had so oppressed me became virtually nonexistent during this period. At every chance I got, armed with the teachings of Mr. Armstrong, I led the charge to convince others that the Catholic Church is evil. I particularly made it my commission to destroy the validity that the Blessed Mother was the queen of anything to anyone who would listen. I would leave literature on how the Blessed Mother was responsible for idolatry by usurping Jesus' authority on car windshields of parishioners attending Sunday Mass. Brainwashed into thinking she was a satanic construct, I cultivated unbelievable hatred towards her.

After Mr. Armstrong's death in the late 80's, his successor failed to stem a political battle over who was the rightful heir of this cult causing the organization to split up into opposing factions. The entire membership was in turmoil because we were terrorized into believing that attending even just one protestant service or Catholic Mass would result in God throwing us into the lake of fire for having committed the unpardonable sin. Having been so intensely indoctrinated into rejecting all the major beliefs of traditional Christianity, it became impossible for many of us to reconcile with a God at all.

Years of being told that if we left this cult we would lose eternal life instilled panic over considering options for worship outside of what we had known. Everyone, including myself, had been convinced that Mr. Armstrong, the self-proclaimed actual second Elijah, would usher in the return of Jesus Christ. It didn't take long for all factions, including the one I had aligned myself with, to splinter even further into offshoots destined for oblivion.

In 2004 I finally realized that the God I clung to under this false religion no longer existed. Feeling overly confused and alienated from traditional Christianity, I opted to become an agnostic and abandon any relationship with God. For the next five years I gave no thought or concern to nurturing a spiritual life. Just being a good person was enough. I was done with religion.

Then in 2009 I started to have these unshakeable feelings to return to the Catholic Church. The more I tried to ignore these urges, the more intense this longing became. I didn't know what to do as I didn't believe in the Blessed Mother, so these feelings weren't rational. To make matters more confusing, the demonic torment that had lain dormant for many years resurfaced. The more I entertained the thought of rediscovering catholism, the worse the nightly torments became. The torment no doubt was a result of fear on the part of demons. My prior interests in various denominations posed no threat to them so they basically left me alone. The Catholic Church however was another story. Demons know the power of Christ that the church inherited. In a last ditch effort they employed the same tactics as before in an attempt to derail my fledging desire to return home to the church. To complicate matters further, I found reluctance on the church's part to acknowledge and get involved in helping me out of this demonic nightmare.

I did have a Catholic friend who stepped out of her comfort zone, and another friend who was a nun, along with her spiritual director (a priest) offering me encouragement and prayers. This spiritual director referred me to a Franciscan monk with experience in dealing with the demonic. Despite him living 300 miles away, it was still close enough that I was able to meet with him in person. He provided invaluable guidance and tools to help me combat my tormentors.

Through the loving efforts of this small "team" and the Holy Spirit, they were able to break through the demonic barrier of staunch opposition to believing in the Blessed Mother . With their continued support and prayers I was eventually able to fully embrace the Catholic faith. It took time and lots of patience, but the closer I drew to the Blessed Mother in heartfelt prayer for deliverance, the more the demonic attacks lessened. I saw the diminishing of the attacks as a positive sign that Our Lady did exist. This sparked a reverence deep within my heart for her title of, "Queen of Heaven". I had rediscovered the love I had for her as a child. With this rediscovery came many spiritual blessings that strengthened my resolve to be victorious over the demonic influences in my life that attempted to derail my coming back into the fold of Christ's church.

When you take a chance and invite her in to your life, the Blessed Mother will make herself known to you. That is what I did. Our Lady made herself known to me in a very special and private way. Out of reverence for her I choose not to disclose the very personal manner in which I came to acknowledge her as the "Queen of Angels".

This also isn't the end of my "story". Throughout the book I will reference some very specific examples of my past demonic experiences as they pertain to the information I will be covering. Know too that my life isn't perfect and all better now. I still face daily struggles to remain in the light of God's love. With the help of heaven and those here on earth who care for me, I can handle this spiritual battle one day at a time.

I would like to end this chapter with a poem I composed on the morning I awoke from my angel dream back in January of 1983. It was my first attempt at praise to God for having rescued my soul from damnation. It was the first time in a long time that I felt deep gratitude and humility.

"Lord You Were Always Right There!"

When my life got rough I went astray,
I should have asked your help instead I turned you away.
I cursed you, and accused you of not wanting to care,
But how was I to know Lord, you were always right there.
And when I cried you cried too,
For all the pain I felt was the pain you knew.
And still you were hurt when you had to see,
The way some others were so unkind to me.
So in my times of deepest despair,
You my Lord Jesus were always right there.
It was through my pain that I was unable to see,
That you had come to my side to share sorrow with me.
You see only the good in me; you know what I am,
For you are my Shepherd and I your lamb,
And a Shepherd guards his flock with care,
So Lord when I cried to for you,
You were already there!

Jan. 14 1983

Chapter 3

Heaven's Warriors

I feel it is prudent to talk about heaven's power over evil before launching right into the world of demons. This way you are grounded in the knowledge that our loving God wouldn't expect you to battle demons without heavenly reinforcements. You are not alone in this spiritual war. I was inspired by the Blessed Mother to write this book as a message of hope from her to you. It doesn't matter whether you are wrestling with literal demons or perhaps just demonic influences in your life, you are not alone! We have heaven's angelic army waiting to assist us in our daily struggles with evil. Our loving God also equipped each and every one of us with super weapons that we can utilize to resist the enemy's personal offensive against us. No special extensive training is required to be able to handle these super weapons. All you need is faith to know that although you may be shouldering the weapon, it is the Lord who will pull the trigger.

No matter how deeply someone is entrenched in the occult, divine deliverance is offered to anyone who asks Our Lady and Jesus for help. God has destined her to be in the forefront of this spiritual war and has placed at her disposal an army of angels. Maybe you are wrestling with an addiction, or are held hostage by a pattern of sin that seems inescapable. While that may not involve the occult, it still involves demonic influences. Satan uses whatever works including human weaknesses to ruin your soul. Jesus and Our Lady don't discriminate; every person regardless of race, religion, or gender will be helped if that person comes to them in full sincerity and humility. Our Lady's love for us as a mother means she sees every one of us as her child which includes non-Catholics and non-Christians too! She has a whole host of angels at her command to help combat the demons that torment you. Her son has already defeated the devil for us, "giving thanks to the Father who has qualified you to share in the inheritance of the saints in the kingdom of light. For he has rescued us from the dominion of darkness and brought us into the kingdom of the Son he loves," (Colossians 1:12–13, NIV). Victory is already ours. All we need to do is claim it.

It is Satan who tries to convince you that he is more powerful than God and that you can't win against him. In Hebrews 2:14 Jesus destroys the devil not for the sake of the angels, but for our sake. Non-Catholics claim that anyone can battle demons on their own if they claim the power of Jesus' name. While there is validity to that when dealing with temptations, I don't recommend it as your only weapon for battling demons or demonic attacks. As I mentioned earlier in the book, while I was a practicing Satanist I delighted in taking on Christian individuals who thought they could rid me of my demons. In every case it was over confidence hidden behind their zealous faith that was their undoing. They felt they didn't need any heavenly warriors other than themselves so they never called in for reinforcements. What they didn't realize was that by going at it alone, they were outnumbered by "my side". It wasn't a one-on-one battle; I had demons beside me who took great pleasure using supernatural powers to manipulate the situation. It is ludicrous to even entertain the fact that humans can battle fallen angels by themselves. Demons don't play fair. As spirit beings they will use weapons that as a mortal you have no access to or defenses against. Why even attempt to take them on alone when heaven's cavalry is just a heartfelt prayer away?

Michael the Archangel along with two thirds of heaven's angels already defeated Satan once before. Satan's utter and complete hold on humanity was shattered on the cross. The Blessed Mother is the Queen of the Angels and will crush the head of Satan some day. They are ALL willing to help fight this battle so why refuse such an opportunity? To struggle alone in a spiritual battle with a demon gives the demon the upper hand. To a demon taking on a lone human without the aid of heaven is like shooting fish in a barrel; no competition. Calling on St. Michael the Archangel will drastically alter the battle in your favor. As Prince of the Heavenly Host his main duty is to wage war against the devil and his minions.

Jesus Became the Ultimate Victor Over Satan

Jesus left heaven and became human so as to be our ultimate sacrifice for all our sins. As John 3:16 (NIV) now so famously states, "For God so loved the world that He gave His one and only Son, that whoever believes in Him shall not perish but have everlasting life." Jesus paid the ultimate sacrifice so that we could be united with God once again. By His resurrection Jesus conquered death allowing us access to go to heaven when we die. This reconciliation in itself was the biggest blow mortally wounding Satan's ability to destroy our soul. In Hebrews 2:14 (NIV) we read, "Inasmuch then as the children have partaken of flesh and blood, He Himself likewise shared the same, that through death He might destroy him who had the power of death, that is, the devil."

Satan thought he had won by having Jesus nailed to a cross. He savored every moment watching our seemingly helpless savior being beaten and whipped beyond recognition by the Roman soldiers. He infused his brutal cruelty into the minds of Jesus' captors so that they shoved a cap full of long piercing thorns on His head all the while mocking Him as a king wearing a crown of thorns. Satan must have exhausted his mind coming up with so much sadistic savagery to hurl at Jesus for the crucifixion. Satan unleashed his full fury against the Son of God that day. However his smug perverted sense of satisfaction disintegrated with Jesus' victory at Calvary.

Jesus hung on the cross for ALL to see. That means the people who were present at the crucifixion site. It also means that the entire spiritual world was a witness to this supreme act of unselfishness. Satan thought Jesus was powerless over the cross because he wouldn't save himself. Satan's grand plan was to make Jesus the object of public ridicule before all the angels and demons. Instead, through the crucifixion, it was Jesus who put Satan on display in front of all the heavenly and demonic forces. Satan had been claiming to both realms that he was created superior as an angel of light. The Holy Angels saw Satan's true nature that afternoon. They saw him not as the powerful Cherubim he insisted he still was, but instead as a foul, corrupt lying murderer. The demonic fallen ones now beheld their great infallible leader as vulnerable and fallible. Satan's plan to publicly humiliate Jesus backfired as it was Satan who was humiliated before the entire spiritual realm. Satan became the public spectacle of defeat before God and all the Heavenly Hosts as well as the entire demonic empire under his command. "And having disarmed principalities and powers, He [Jesus] made a public spectacle of them, triumphing over them by the cross" (Colossians 2:15).

Make Jesus Real

I have heard well meaning people who wanted to offer me comfort during some demonic trial say time and time again, "I know what you must be feeling", or "I know what you are going through". The reality is that if you haven't gone through that experience, you have no idea what it is like. Compassion and empathy are born out of experience. If I encountered and had to help a frightened pregnant woman who went into labor in front of me, and I told her I know what she must be feeling, I would be lying. I have never had children so I don't have a clue what it feels like to give birth. I am sure that poor woman would feel a whole lot better if another woman who had children of her own assisted her.

Have you ever been bullied, ridiculed, accused of things you didn't say or do, lied to, rejected by your peers, tempted by Satan, or betrayed by a close friend? During those darkest moments didn't you wish you had someone who knew exactly what you were going through? Since God was never human he never experienced human emotions, but in allowing His only Son united with God to become human, Jesus experienced the entire range of human emotions. Jesus became one of us. His human existence gave our Messiah a first hand deep understanding of all the pain and sorrow we experience. Jesus is truly qualified to say to you, "I know what it feels like". Jesus knows how conniving and cunning Satan is in his temptations. He battled Satan and demons all throughout His ministry. Whenever we come under a demonic attack or temptation, Jesus with His perfect memory remembers what it felt like when he was mortal. His overflowing empathy and compassion for your struggles because of that memory is genuine and real. As important as the title King of all Kings is in all the cosmos, Jesus will always make and take the time to personally listen and comfort you. Jesus carried His cross to Calvary and now He offers to carry you when you can't stand up against the evil ones. Make Jesus real by removing Him from the cross and placing Him in your heart. Ask for His help.

The Blessed Mother, Queen of the Angels

Luke 1:48 states that all generations to come will call her blessed. In the magnificat Our Lady said that her soul "magnifies" the Lord. Just like a magnifying glass, to magnify means to enlarge and make something clearer. Non-Catholics accuse us Catholics of "Mary worship" taking emphasis away from Jesus. Her soul magnifies the Lord. She wants to help make God and her son clearer to you and me. Revelation 12:1 pictures her as a woman clothed with the sun, with a moon under her feet, and a crown of twelve stars over her head. She has been given power over the devil by God! God has given her command over the angels to deploy them to people who sincerely ask for her intervention. She sends help whenever help is needed.

Our Lady is especially hated by Satan because she is a woman. Satan took great pleasure in causing Eve the first woman ever created, to sin. Satan gloated over man's fall from grace which followed Eve's transgression. From that point on Satan perpetuated the myth that women are the weaker sex and inferior to man. Imagine his fury when Mary accepts God's calling to become the human mother of the redeemer of mankind. Satan tries to destroy this holy infant through Herod's decree to kill all male children less than two years of age. Mary and her husband Joseph escape this genocide with the <u>help</u> <u>of</u> <u>the</u> <u>angels</u>. Even the mother of God couldn't have escaped the devil's wrath without divine angelic intervention.

You have to remember with Satan this is personal. Mary became the second Eve when she accepted God's calling. Satan is humiliated by Mary's unyielding commitment to follow God's will. The angel Gabriel said that the Lord IS with her meaning constantly around during her earthly stay. I hardly doubt that when she went to heaven that status changed. Gabriel didn't say, "The Lord is competing with you". The Lord IS with you, meaning that God, Jesus, and Mary are working together for our salvation. She is with her son Jesus now.

Satan is so enraged by this apparent humiliation that he has declared all out war against her. He has gone to extremes to discredit her. Calling on all those he deceived through false doctrines, 'protest'–ants lead his charge in attempting to discredit any attempt to utilize her as a weapon against the demons. Just look at how venomous the attacks are in the publications that claim devotion to the Blessed Mother is idolatry. Venom comes from poisonous snakes, and Satan did manifest as a serpent to Eve. Don't hate the authors of such publications for they are deceived by Satan. Pray for them instead because she still loves them as much as she loves you. No one is beyond redemption in this life!! View these attacks on the Blessed Mother by non-Catholics as positive proof that Satan is so terrified of her that he will stop at nothing to keep us away from her love and protection. Never forget that when we invite Our Lady in to our heart, she will make herself known to each of us in a different but personal way. You don't need to receive an apparition or visitation from the Blessed Mother to know that she is real and working in your life. All you have to do is have faith and trust in her all encompassing perfect motherly love. As our loving mother she loves you and me just as much as if she had given birth to each one of us. A loving mother doesn't ignore the cries of her children.

Angels:
Heaven's Warriors and Our Personal Guardians

Angels are first mentioned in Genesis when Cherubim (a class of angels) were placed as protectors at Eden's gate after the fall of Adam and Eve. From that point on angelic heavenly beings appear throughout the Old and New Testaments either aiding, or bringing messages from God to mankind.

It was an angel that led Lot and his family out from Sodom during its destruction. It was an angel that stayed the hand of Abraham as he was going to sacrifice Isaac his son. Jacob actually spent the entire night physically wrestling with an angel. It was the archangel Gabriel who brought the message to Mary that she would bear our savior, and it was an angel that helped the apostle Peter escape prison. In the gospel of Luke, an anguished Jesus is comforted and encouraged by an angel shortly before his arrest.

So what is the nature of angels? Psalm 103 in verse 20 explains their nature, "Praise the Lord you His angels, you mighty ones who do God's bidding" (NIV). Angels not only praise God but they carry out his will. Angels are dispatched to earth as both guardians of man and messengers. God has given the heavenly angels the commission to watch over us. Psalm 91:11 (NIV), "For He will command His angels concerning you to guard you in all your ways". The book of Hebrews not only confirms this verse but also sheds light on their purpose, "Are not all angels ministering spirits sent to serve those who will inherit salvation?" (NIV). Angels are all around us all the time. Seeing as they are messengers, they not only bring messages from heaven to us, but also carry our prayers back to heaven.

There are different types or groups of angels. Although all angels praise and serve God, each group has it's own specific purpose in carrying out God's will for the universe and mankind. There actually is a heavenly hierarchy. In the fifth century one of the early Christian scholars by the name of Pseudo–Dionysius wrote a book called, "On the Heavenly Hierarchy". Here he organized the angelic ranks into nine distinct groups, broken down into three triads containing three types of angels. This is not defined Catholic doctrine and some confusion exists over what category of angels belongs where. Despite the various opinions among theologians, the listing I am providing is the most widely held belief today. I went through the bible and added some scriptural references that mention each angelic rank specifically. This way it helps you understand where Pseudo–Dionysius found evidence of this hierarchy.

The Nine Choirs of Angels
First Triad– surround God's throne.
1. Seraphim
2. Cherubim
3. Thrones

Seraphim are the angels closest to God and are beings of perfect light. They are mentioned in Isaiah 6, verse 2 and again in verse 6.

Cherubim are full of knowledge. Ezekiel was only one of a

few people to ever see Cherubim. Read Ezekiel chapter 1 and chapter 10 to get an idea of how compelling and powerful they are. Also see Exodus 25:19–20, Exodus 37:6–9, I Samuel 4:4, II Samuel 6:2, and Kings 6:23–28. As part of the first triad, Cherubim surround God's throne. Ezekiel sees them in his vision as extremely commanding beings. They were the ones who wielded the flaming swords guarding the gates of Eden after the expulsion of Adam and Eve.

The image of these magnificent beings has been defiled by the evil ones. Satan and his fallen angels have perverted the image of Cherubim into chubby naked little rosy–cheeked babies commonly depicted in religious art throughout the centuries. The visual of adorably vulnerable and delicate winged naked babies emasculates the importance of their rank. I know this view may come across to you as harsh, offensive, and perhaps even an exaggerated scrutiny of something insignificant. Cuddly little cherubs after all look so non-threatening. That is exactly my point. It is another overt ploy by Satan to discredit God's power. Why? Because Satan can't stand the fact that he wasn't as powerful against the angels as his pride led him to believe. Satan is attempting to mock God by deceiving us into accepting a visual representation of one of God's most mighty beings as nothing more than a frail baby with wings. This is a clandestine deception designed to reduce our concept of some of the majesty and awe that encircles God's throne. This depiction of a cherub is a blatant contradiction of how they are described in the Bible. Maybe you are thinking that embracing such a representation of a cherub is harmless. Deception of any sort and to any degree is, at its core, still a lie, and that is never harmless! I am not advocating that we should wage a protest against all visual representations of cherubs. All I am asking you is to acknowledge the origin of this image and realize its creation stems from a fallen angel who is consumed with 100% pure jealousy.

Thrones are angels of pure humility, peace, and submission. Thrones are mentioned by St. Paul in Colossians 1:16, "For by Him were all things created that are in heaven, and that are in earth, visible and invisible, whether they be Thrones, Dominions, Principalities, or Powers: all things were created by Him and for Him" (KJV).

Second Triad – carries out instructions from the first triad as well as governs over the earth and universe as a whole.
1. Dominions
2. Virtues
3. Powers

Dominions make known and carry out orders given by God.

Virtues provide strength and courage and oversee miracles as well as govern all of nature.

Powers protect heaven and us from evil. They are known as warrior angels. St. Paul in Ephesians 1:21 and Colossians 1:16 mentions Powers, Dominions, Principalities, and Thrones.

Third Triad – most concerned with daily life on earth.
1. Principalities
2. Archangels
3. Angels

Principalities look after continents, nations, and cities (Colossians 1:16).

Archangels are our messengers as well as protectors. Three are named in the bible: Michael (Revelation 12:7), Gabriel (Luke 1:26–28, Daniel 8:15–16), and Raphael (Tobit 5:3–4, 6:1–

4, 11:4–14, 12:15–18).

Angels are the closest to the material world and us. They can be our guardian angel as well as deliver our prayers to God. Jesus in his parable of the lost sheep tells us that we each have our own personal angel, "See that you do not look down on one of these little ones. For I tell you that **their** angels in heaven always see the face of my Father in heaven" (Matthew 18:10, NIV). A God of love would never send his children into a world presently dominated by Satan and the fallen ones alone. In His infinite wisdom he assigns a guardian angel to every baby at conception to keep watch over them all throughout their life from birth to death. Angels are all around us every minute of the day and night. Their help is always available if we have the faith and courage to let them in our life. It is an angel in Revelation 20:1–3 who descends from heaven with a great chain to shackle Satan and lock him up in the bottomless pit in the future.

Our spiritual development is of the utmost importance and a priority to our angel. God informs each guardian angel of the spiritual lessons we need to experience in order to grow in His love. They then will guide people into our life to help us in this spiritual journey. There are no chance or random people encounters in your life. Everything happens for a reason. Through these people we experience situations and circumstances that allow us to embrace Godly attributes. Whether it is a life–long meaningful friendship or just a random smile and kind word to the person standing in line behind you at the grocery checkout, you are offered the opportunity to embrace a Christ like attitude. Even people who cause our worst experiences are guided into our life because during a trial of great anguish, it allows us to reach deep within our soul to pull out a strength we never believed existed to deal with the crisis. Virtues are born out of adversity if you allow the adversity to draw you closer to God. NO ONE IS EVER IN YOUR LIFE BY MISTAKE!!

Remember God made you and is in charge of your life's design; guardian angels are His messengers sent to help and assist you to recognize this potential. They are also here to protect us from undo harm. Just as demons can influence our thoughts to make the wrong choice, angels too can influence our thoughts to make the right choice.

One way guardian angels protect us is through intuition. Passengers who at the last minute decided not to board a doomed flight attributed their action to an intuitive sense of impending peril. More than likely it was their guardian angel influencing their thought processes telling them not to get on the plane. Coincidences and synchronicity are manifestations of angelic interventions in our life. Have you ever avoided a serious tragedy or circumstance because of a string of seemingly random coincidences? Don't chalk it up to a piece of good luck but thank God and your guardian angel for orchestrating these coincidences so as to avert a personal disaster.

If everything is going wrong in your life and you seem to have a run of bad luck, it may be fallen angels creating havoc, or it may be a good angel giving you subtle signs that you are going down the wrong path. God instructs your guardian angel to place obstacles in front of you that force you to stop and rethink your priorities if you stray too far from what God intends for you. This is very important to understand. Not all the bad things we experience are the result of demonic tampering. Sometimes God instructs our guardian angel to deliver a warning message in the only form that we are most receptive to; obstacles.

There is an ancient Hebrew legend that was taught to young children regarding personal angels. It is said that there is a grain of truth in every legend. While I can't vouch for its validity, it comes close to a concept I have always believed in. I believe that everyone is created in love. God is love and since God creates us it doesn't matter how we were humanly conceived. We were thought up out of love by God. There is this connection to God right from conception. Young children before they experience the ugliness the world inflicts on them reflect that closeness to God by virtue of their innocence, sense of trust, and willingness to engage strangers. Even as life tears apart that inner God connection over time, we still have this intense hunger and searching for a greater meaning to the purpose of life. Once we understand that what is missing in our life is a relationship with God, we once again seek to reunite ourselves with Him. Despite what life throws at us, the connection to God we felt at the beginning of our existence is embedded deep within our soul longing to re–establish that union.

This is the ancient teaching of the Talmud once taught to children long ago on the God connection with the unborn. While still in the womb God appoints an angel as personal guardian over the unborn child. This angel as a messenger of God conveys to the unborn child all the secrets of the universe, creation, and heaven during the nine month gestation period. Then just before the moment of birth the angel kisses the baby above the upper lip. This creates the indentation just below the nose and above the upper lip that we all have. This mark symbolizes God's love for every person on earth. This mark also is a reminder that every human being is aware of God's divine wisdom. The angel's kiss just before birth erases all conscious memory of what was taught in the womb. All throughout life however, when someone hears some truth that resonates profoundly within their soul, it taps into the subconscious where those angelic lessons haven't been erased. These truths that really hit home in our heart help to remind us that our connection to God hasn't been completely severed.

Finally, remember that angels fight alongside us in our spiritual battle against the forces of darkness. Michael as an Archangel can be compared to David, and Lucifer the Cherubim, to the giant Goliath. In a battle of mismatched strengths against a much mightier being, Michael came out the victor and cast the Devil out of heaven. This proves that strength is not the source of power; purity is. Fallen angels are no match for heavenly angels filled with holiness. The Blessed Mother who is Queen of the Angels will always dispatch these spiritual warriors to fight when you can't. All you have to do is ask! Call upon Her and all the heavenly hosts when you sense you are under attack from the Evil One.

Michael the Archangel is a profound figure found in not only the Christian faith, but also in Islamic and Jewish faiths. Call upon him when you feel under spiritual attack. Write the following prayer down on a piece of paper and carry it with you, or memorize it. Recite it as soon as you sense danger of any sort.

"Saint Michael the Archangel, defend us in battle.
Be our protection against the wickedness
and snares of the devil.
May God rebuke him, we humbly pray; and do Thou,
O Prince of the Heavenly host by the Divine Power of God,
cast into hell Satan and all the evil spirits who roam
throughout the world seeking the ruin of souls."

When the Saints Go Marching In

The more we embrace the powerful role of God, Jesus, the Blessed Mother, angels, and Saints in spiritual combat, the more we understand how important their assistance in our lives becomes. We Catholics are constantly unfairly accused by the Protestant community of elevating righteous dead people (Saints) over the authority of God by asking in prayer for their assistance instead of God's. The thought of praying for help to a Saint instead of Jesus is seen by them as idolatry. Let's take a look at clarifying this misconception.

First of all, what is a Saint? Saints are part of the mystical body of Christ. We as part of the mystical body of Christ will become saints someday when we arrive in heaven. A "Saint" is just an ordinary person called to do an extra–ordinary thing throughout their life that magnifies God's purpose for us on a grander scale. Such a person is graced with an extra measure of character and resolve to endure intense suffering and even martyrdom at times because of their faith. These are individuals who by exemplifying heavenly virtues under great adversity develop deep holiness while still on earth. Most of them are betrayed in varying degrees by people within the faith. St. Theresa of Avila was a nun who despite her deep devotion to the Lord was falsely accused and brought before the Inquisition three times! Despite the agony of friends and the church turning on her, she did not waiver in the commission God gave her. Instead she grew closer to God and wrote some of the most inspiring writings regarding spirituality.

Two of my favorite Saints are St. John Vianney and Padre Pio because they literally battled demons on a daily basis. Padre Pio sustained severe bruising from his demonic attackers. Father Vianney endured demonic physical assaults during the night that ranged from objects flying around the room to actually being physically tossed out of bed by demons. They even set fire to his bed while he was in it! The demons were very angry at him because of his deep commitment to the sacrament of confession. I know personally how unnerving demonic attacks are, yet Father Vianney would, not only accept it as part of his sufferings, but also make light of it. Sometimes his guests would witness such demonic activity and be afraid. He would very calmly explain that that such torment meant that he would hear a great confession the next day. Both men despite the incredible almost impossible relentless retaliation from Satan drew closer to God. Not everyone has that kind of strength. It takes a very special person to willingly and freely accept such a path. Most people would buckle after experiencing just one such demonic attack, never mind enduring it for a lifetime. For me these men are an inspiration on how to handle myself when faced with very similar spiritual trials.

Catholics don't worship Saints for that is idolatry. Instead, we view them as heroes, someone we can look up to. People we can look up to, who were just as human as we are, and subjected to all the human and spiritual trials we face even today. They are people who despite the odds didn't waiver or back down when it came to serving God. We all need heroes and we all need role models. Our children today tend to gravitate to "heroes" whose claim to fame is based on stardom and wealth. These individuals despite a lack of virtues that all too often leads to public scandals are esteemed by our youth because of a "rags to riches" story. Character for today's youth is measured by the amount of money such an individual makes, and not on Godly principles. Many such human "idols" fade away into obscurity once they have exhausted all their physical talents. The legacy of the heavenly Saints endures forever.

Praying to a Saint isn't idolatry. The confusion surrounding this concept comes from the Elizabethan era where "pray" was a commonly used expression. "I pray thee that thou wouldst show me the way to town" in modern language would translate to, "I am requesting or asking you to show me the way to town." An expression still used today is, "Pray tell". "Pray tell, what did he do this time"? Pray tell simply means "do tell". During the time King James commissioned his version of the bible to be written, the phrase "to pray" meant to ask or request. So to pray to a Saint simply means you are asking them something and not worshiping them.

It would really help to shed the myth that when we die and go to heaven we will sit on our own puffy white cloud dressed in a white robe and playing a harp for all eternity. When we get to heaven we will be with God. We will finally fully understand God's great purpose and plan for humanity. We will look down from heaven and see people on earth through the eyes of God. Saints who went above and beyond in this life to serve others still carry that desire into heaven. That desire transforms into intercessory prayer for us. Being immortal means not needing to eat or sleep allowing them to pray on our behalf 24/7 without ceasing. Saints were once human beings. They overcame their obstacles through an intense prayer life. They know the power of prayer and are willing to pray to God with you. Humbly asking a Saint for intercessory prayer isn't worshiping or glorifying them. It is a request that they gladly will respond to.

The Saint Who Intervened on My Behalf
In the spring of 2010 the urge to return to the Catholic Church was overwhelming. Trying to come back to the church of my childhood wasn't easy for me given all the

anti–Catholic rhetoric I had been subjected to while in the WCG cult. Unbeknownst to me God was calling me home for two reasons. The first reason was because He missed me. He missed all those long conversations I used to have with Him every day while still a child. He was reaching out to me even though I didn't recognize it at the time. The second reason I was called back was to write this very book of hope so as to reach those lost souls who want to break free from the occult but don't know how.

I sought the help of a young priest who understood my unique situation. His compassionate demeanor tore down my walls of distrust. As we became good friends I began to integrate back into the church. About this time I became plagued with demonic attacks reminiscent of what I went through decades ago. The demons were attempting to thwart my return because they already knew that I would write this book and they didn't want to see that. My spiritual life went into crisis and this priest vowed he would never abandon me and asked me to trust him, which I did. Then one fateful day after Mass he approached me and very coldly said that he was breaking off immediately all contact with me forever. He refused to give any reason and just walked away. To me he was my close friend and this betrayal ripped my heart to shreds. I was abandoned during my darkest hour. My agonizing hurt turned into anger almost instantly. I left the church vowing revenge by giving in to the demonic pressure I was under to return to evil ways.

I hated God because I didn't understand why He asked me to return to the church only to feel such painful rejection and abandonment. On my own I was powerless to contain the demonic activity affecting my life. If the Blessed Mother had appeared to me in person at that moment I would have rejected her too because she was the mother of God and my soul was in so much agony. I turned back to the occult for help in handling the demonic. I signed up for a summer mediumship development class at a Spiritualist camp. I wanted to be as far away from God as possible. I assumed that by hiding in the realm of the occult He would never look or find me there.

The Spiritualist camp was a good three hours away from my home. Located right by the ocean, it was a perfect location for spiritual retreats because there wasn't much human activity going on. I had no one to talk to because the camp was generally empty during the week. The twelve week course was held on Tuesday evenings so I would stay overnight in one of their little guest rooms rather than drive home late at night. On the first night I signed up I noticed a bookcase by the front entrance full of used books for sale. It was filled with all sorts of books on reincarnation, astral projection, channeling, shamanism, and every other aspect of the occult. Since the guest rooms were austere with no amenities such as television or radio, I decided to buy a used book to read before going to bed.

The very first book I laid my hands on was a book written by a nun on the life of St. Theresa of Avila. Stunned, I searched the entire bookcase for any other religious books and found none. Why on earth was this lone book about the life of a Catholic Saint tucked away amidst the multitude of occult books? Initially I was reluctant to buy it because everything I had read about Saints when I was in parochial school made Saints appear unblemished and holy from the day of their birth. I didn't want to read about yet another Saint's perfect spiritual life which would only intensify my self-hatred. Still, the unnatural location of this book peaked my curiosity enough compelling me to buy it.

In the stillness of my room I opened the book. It contained excerpts from the various writings of St. Theresa. I was half expecting to read a white washed sanitized account of her life. Instead her words spoke about the spiritual conflict and turmoil she experienced early on. She wrote about her struggle with vanity. Her words mirrored how I was feeling. I saw so much of me in her struggles that I finally felt connected to someone who knew what I felt. Unable to put down the book I read on and came to the part where she found a close friend, a priest named Gracian. Their friendship meant the world to her. Somewhere along the line though, her dearest friend believed the false accusations by the church against her. He abruptly and callously ended their long time friendship. Her writings reflected the agony of this betrayal and terrible loss as she tried to make sense of it. Having just lost my friend in a similar fashion, her words expressed my emotions. I identified with so many of her personal struggles. I began to admire her tenacity to fight through her humanness to grow close to God. Reading the book cracked open the door of my heart to the possibility of reconciling with God someday. Before I drifted off to sleep I called out to St. Theresa challenging her to prove to me that she was in fact reaching out to me.

On my way home the following morning the first church I drove by was named St. Theresa. I stopped at a second hand shop shortly thereafter and stumbled onto the only prayer card in the entire shop tucked in among the stationery items. The prayer card was to St. Theresa. I then came to a secular bookstore in the next town over that was going out of business and decided to check it out. The sale banner advertised 75% off all remaining books. As I walked in I was disappointed to see most of the book shelves empty. Only one large table remained with the picked over rejects. On the table one book was propped up against wall. The title in huge white lettering against a midnight blue background read, "Dark Night of the Soul" written by St. John of the Cross. He was very close to St. Theresa and the two of them enjoyed a deep spiritual friendship. This book was the only religious book among a mish mash of books on secular topics. St. Theresa of Avila had proved to me through these signs that she was real.

What I didn't realize at the time was that the loss of my friend was the catalyst launching me into a deeper relationship with my Creator. I had come to rely too heavily on human intervention to save my soul from the demons that were tormenting me. With my priest friend out of my life, there was no church support to come to my aid. In my hurt I rejected God because I too wanted Him to feel the agony of being abandoned by someone He Loved. I am convinced that St. Theresa of Avila witnessed all of this from heaven. Knowing my heart was closed to God she offered to try to intercede on His behalf. By guiding me to find and read her book she was able to break through the barrier of my emotional pain through shared experiences. It was through her writings that I realized that the only one who could save me from myself was God. I had to stop looking around for help and start looking up to heaven for deliverance. I became inspired by St. Theresa's personal journey of spirituality. It was her book that made me realize that nothing we experience in life should ever separate us from loving God. It was her intervention that opened the door for me to re-establish a relationship with God.

Chapter 4

Satan's Army

I spent a few agonizing nights in prayer asking for guidance on just how much information should be included in explaining the hierarchy of hell. In this day and age of the internet with various search engines, one can Google just about any word to find a virtual cornucopia of information on any subject. My intent is not to give you nightmares on just how organized and powerful Satan's army is, but to create a deep respect for how potent our opponent can be.

Even in the dark or black arts, those who call up demons are mindful of the hierarchy and dare not attempt to summon certain classes of demons. This is an extremely serious book about an extremely serious situation. We are at war! Souls are at stake! Today many people, including Christian believers, have a fuzzy and vague concept of what comprises The Evil One's army. A big misconception regarding Satan's storm troopers is the notion that demons wander around aimlessly in a disorganized fashion with just Satan as their leader. Hell's army isn't some punkish street gang. That couldn't be further from the truth. I will be stressing repeatedly throughout this book the crucial fact that one of Satan's greatest strategies is to deceive the world into believing he and his minions doesn't exist. By doing so people are unaware of these presences so they don't put up any defenses to stop them. Prayer recited specifically to protect us from the snares of the devil becomes a powerful impenetrable defense.

Confusion even among satanic groups runs rampant over which demons hold what demonic office, who is who, and who does what. Satan wants to keep his hierarchy cloaked in ambiguity so that they go undetected by us. The first order or upper echelon demons go to great lengths not to be identified. They know once we discover their identity we can call on Jesus, the Blessed Mother, and Holy Angels to help us chase them away.

The good news is that although one third of the angels fell with Lucifer, they are still outnumbered 2 to 1 by heaven's angels. That puts the odds in our favor. In the end demons will be permanently cast into hell, ("And the Devil who deceived them, was thrown into the lake of burning sulfur, where the beast and the false prophet had been thrown. They will be tormented day and night forever and ever". Revelation 20:10, NIV). If you are in the midst of a spiritual battle, please remember that there are more good angels than bad ones. In the end we win.

It's bad enough that our enemy is an unseen force. It is very dangerous to engage an enemy if you don't even know who they are. Convincing yourself that your mind can't deal with this entire concept won't make them go away; in fact it draws them nearer. Making assumptions on their capabilities based on pop culture and Hollywood movies is inviting disaster. There is a saying that knowledge is power. Gaining insight on who and what demons are, shouldn't give you a sense of power, but create a deep desire to drop to your knees in daily heartfelt prayer to be delivered from their influences.

I recently read a book on spiritual warfare by a well meaning minister. In the chapter where he described the ranks of hell, I almost fell out of my chair. He was so far off from the truth as to the order of demons. He relegated Beelzebub to the rank of lower level spirit who we have to deal with daily. Beelzebub is the "prince of demons" (Matthew 12:34, NIV), second in command to Satan himself. He is so powerful, that in many black art circles, attempting to conjure him would result in that person's death. He generally doesn't make house calls.

Never underestimate what we are up against! Trust me, I know from firsthand experience, the higher the rank, the more dangerous and deceitful they are. Even in ritual magic while conjuring up a demon it is understood that the conjurer NEVER step a foot out of the magic circle during such rites, no matter how scared one becomes. Why? Because the more powerful demons will use trickery and fear to lure someone out of the circle's "protection". If they succeed then the bargain struck is null and void and the demon collects his "prize" which is the person's soul right there and then. Make no mistake about it; messing with demons isn't child's play. There is no "do over" if things go terribly wrong. On the bright side, the average person, Catholic, or Protestant, won't be involved with such high level demons anyway unless they have been involved in the deeper levels of the occult. Still don't breathe a sigh of relief just yet. There are plenty of lesser demons that invade our space waiting for you to knowingly or unknowingly invite them in closer.

The demonic world mirrors the heavenly world but as an opposite. Instead of the nine choirs of angels there are the nine types of demons. I want to stress that the following list isn't absolute. The order of demons varies among the satanic community. The list I included comes from what I was familiarized with when I was a neophyte. As a 'neophyte' (initiate) it was required memorization for me.

WARNING:
PLEASE READ THIS DISCLAIMER BEFORE PROCEEDING ON WITH THE CHAPTER!

The following information contains very specific details about individual demons. The names I have selected are popular within the teenage goth movement. You may never have heard of any of these names, but chances are, teens gravitating to this anti–Christian movement have! Parents and teachers especially need to be aware of the danger such exposure can result in to a young adult. Since this information is readily available through the internet I feel it is much safer to read what bare minimum you need to be forearmed from a book published by a Catholic source. There are some websites run by Satanists or evil influenced individuals who have placed a curse or spell on anyone who visits their site. Curiosity to learn more can result in a demonic attachment obtained by searching the web for specific demons. THE ONLY PEOPLE WHO REALLY KNOW THE NAMES OF DEMONS NOT MENTIONED IN THE BIBLE ARE THOSE WHO PRACTICE OR HAVE PRACTICED BLACK MAGIC!!!! (With the exception of priests trained in exorcism).

Nine Types of Demons

1. **False gods** – high ranking demons who managed to get nations and peoples to worship them as gods such as Baal, Astarte, Moloch, and Thamuz to name a few.
2. **Lying spirits**
3. **Iniquitous spirits**
4. **Vengeful spirits**
5. **Deluding spirits**
6. **Creators of tempests**
7. **Furies**
8. **Accusers**
9. **Tempters**

Demon of the Month Club

Demonologists, including myself, generally agree that the best times to contact the demon of your choosing is during the month they are most active. This is the time when they are the most active in spreading their brand of evil and most receptive to your invocations. Please note that this list isn't absolute, but is the most commonly held view by the majority of Satanists. Demons are dishonest by nature so these might not even be the right names of the demon in charge for that month.

January – Belial
February – Leviathan
March – Satan
April – Astarte
May – Lucifer
June – Baalberith
July – Beelzebub
August – Astaroth
September – Thamuz
October – Baal

November – Hecarte
December – Moloch

If some of these names sound familiar it is because they were once worshiped as a god in ancient times. The Old Testament makes mention of some of these gods (demons) being worshipped by the enemies of Israel.

Besides the nine groups of demons there are many various other classes of demons such as Familiar spirits, Incubus, Succubus and the four Crown Princes' of hell. On top of that demons hold various titles such as: Princes, Ministers, Ambassadors, Justices, Chancellor of hell, Grand Dukes, Marquis of hell, and Counts. It isn't important to understand the infernal makeup of these positions. All demons are 100% evil, and all demons no matter where on the charts they rank, are out to destroy your soul. It is really just a matter of degrees (no pun intended).

Demon All–Stars:
The Top Ten List
Even the demon world has its superstar class of demons. They are very popular names that are becoming even popular, partly due to the rise of the Goth movement of our teens. I used to be a Goth "metal head" as recent as 2011 and some of the bands I listened to like "Cradle of Filth", "Avenged Sevenfold", "Incubus", and "Rotting Christ", to name a few, wrote songs about demons. Many of these metal bands actually name demons and pay homage to them in their lyrics. The whole Goth movement emphasizes rebellion against all things Christian and traditional and glorifies death and destruction. Our young adults are being victimized by demons unknowingly through brainwashing via songs. I will discuss this more in a later chapter. For now

my goal here is to list some of the more common names being put out there, and to give you their title because young adults are learning about them through this style of music.

Beelzebub – Lord of the flies, once the god of the Philistines. Matthew, Mark, and Luke refer to him as the leader of the demons, Matthew 12:24–27; Mark 3:22; Luke 11:15–19. Matthew 12:24 refers to him as "prince of the devils". He is second in command under Satan. Satanic tradition claims that he once belonged to the order of cherubim. He ranks number one in under the false god category. He is extremely powerful and not concerned with the individual so much, as opposed to targeting large masses of people such as ethnic groups and nations. Generally he doesn't except personal invites but will send one of his underlings to do his bidding for him. I do want to note that on internet sites I actually came across groups who worship him and speak of invoking him. As an ex–Satanist I cannot stress enough that if someone manages to actually get him to appear it may result in that person's untimely death because he is so powerful.

Belial – One of the four crown princes' of hell. Satanic tradition believes him to have once been the prince of the order of Virtues. In 2 Corinthians 6:15, (NIV) Paul makes the association that Belial is a very powerful demon "what harmony is there between Christ and Belial?" Belial is also spoken of in the Old Testament in Deuteronomy 13:13; Judges, 19:22 and 20:13; 1 Samuel 1:16, 2:12, 10:27, 30:22; 2 Samuel 16:7, 20:1, 23:6; 1 Kings 21:10–13; 2 Chronicles 13:7. He is the demon one summons if they want to get ahead in this life and gain prestige and material wealth. He also is associated with independence and having no masters, a favorite of rebellious teens.

Leviathan – Grand admiral of hell, one of the four crown prince's of hell. Satanic tradition claims that he once belonged to the order of Cherubim and that he is the link to twisted subconscious thoughts and dreams.

Set – Once the Egyptian Lord of the darkness, satanic tradition claims he is one of the seven sons of Satan. This demon today has his own worshipping cult known as "The Temple of Set". Followers are called "Setians".
v
Thoth – A very important demon, also one of Satan's seven sons. He is the master trickster and very brilliant which makes him an opposing foe because he likes to outsmart humans intellectually.

Asmodeus – Christian tradition lists him as the king of demons. Satanic tradition claims he is originally from the first triad of good angels. He is the demon responsible for lust and sexual perversions. His specialty is to break up marriages and relationships. It has been believed within satanic circles that he can confer the power to read minds to his human followers. Asmodeus is the named demon in Tobit 3:8

Azreal – The Jewish tradition claims he is the full embodiment of evil but does God's work as the angel of death. Satanic tradition claims that he was once part of the order of Cherubim.

A note on the seven sons of Satan. I could not find any real references to this concept outside of the satanic world. I did find through the internet that Marvel comics had a comic book series about a son of Satan. It came out in the 1970's I did not research what exactly this comic was about but I remember seeing some classmates of mine reading it during recess times. I remember seeing the glossy eye catching comic covers as a kid.

1 John 3:10 (NIV) references children of the devil; "This is how we know who the children of God are and who the children of the devil are..." Also in the gospel of John, Jesus addresses the Jews and 8:44 we read, "You belong to your father the Devil, and you want to carry out your father's desires" (NIV). There is no mention anywhere in the bible about seven particular sons. In satanic culture there is too much deviation on which the seven sons are so I didn't bother with including a list of possible suspects.

Baphomet – Often mistaken for Satan because he is the half human, half goat with a goat's head demon that is used in satanic worship. Neo–pagan witches or wiccans DO NOT worship the devil or this demon. He is represented as a sitting, legs crossed figure with cloven hooves, a man's upper torso, black wings, and a goat's head. The Church of Satan which I affiliated with for a short while back in the 1970's adopted a sigil of Baphomet that has a goat's head inside of an inverted pentagram, with Hebrew figures that spell out Leviathan. On the forehead of this demon is a star which represents that Lucifer was once called the "morning star". It was not only placed behind the altar but also worn as a medallion by followers. It is the most commonly seen and adopted symbol of devil worship today. The inverted pentagram distinguishes the difference between a satanic worshipper and a witch whose pentagram is not inverted, but is just a 5 pointed star within a circle. When the pentagram is inverted (rotated upside down) the star now appears to resemble a goat's head with two horns.

Incubus – Actually it is a type of demon as opposed to a specific entity with a name. It is a sex demon that visits women at night. Mainly a feared monster back in the Middle Ages, today thanks again to the Goth genre, it is making a comeback with our youth.

Succubus – It is the counterpart to the Incubus, attacking men at night. These demons can manifest as either male or female at will. Both types are being revered by the youth Goths because it glorifies lustful sex without consequences (STD's and pregnancy). The common expression heard among these youths regarding Incubi and Sucubi is (and please excuse the crudeness of it), "getting a lay without having to pay".

In addition it is noteworthy to mention the four crown prince's of hell as made popular today.
1. **Satan**
2. **Belial**
3. **Leviathan**
4. **Lucifer**

This list is based solely on satanic traditions and not biblical references. There is quite a bit of confusion over whether Lucifer is a separate demon from Satan.

I also want to bring to your attention two demons that have latched onto our young children's play time. While kids everywhere have innocently spoken these words at least once or twice during their playtime, it is still music to the demon's ears. It is a way they remain alive and active deep within a child's subconscious without being discovered. It opens a door albeit a small one for other evil entities to indoctrinate children into a world of demonic influences.

There is an Indian demon called Rakshasa who physically attacks unsuspecting people eating them alive, but he will also eat dead people. To rid yourself of such a demon one must cry out "uncle". How many times have you heard children cry "uncle" when they wanted to stop inflicted rough housing by another playmate? Crying uncle is the way in Indian tradition to chase this demon away. While you may see it as just a harmless child's phrase, it still acknowledges a demon's existence. Demons aren't fussy. They will gladly accept crumbs like this.

The second demon children tend to invoke unwittingly revolves around magic. It is the demon Abraxas who in ancient Egypt was considered a supreme god and source of divine emanations. Saying "Abracadabra" while doing some magic trick is in fact calling upon Abraxas. Again just child's play, but it is planting a seed in their minds.

If that isn't scary enough, demons and Satan can impersonate good angels. "For such are false apostles, deceitful workers, transforming themselves into the apostles of Christ. And no marvel; for Satan himself is transformed into an angel of light." (1 Corinthians 11:13–15, KJV). 1 Timothy 4:1, (KJV), mentions yet another type of demon, "Now the spirit speaks expressively, that in the latter times some shall depart from the faith, giving heed to seducing spirits and doctrines of devils".

These are the demons that twist scriptural truth's just enough so that they are still believable. They perpetuate various brands of Christianity that are nothing more than sugar coated lies.

When I converted from Satanism to Christianity I fell into a religious cult that best describes what was meant in 1 Timothy 4:1. I was a follower of Herbert W. Armstrong and his church, the World Wide Church of God. He claimed to be an actual apostle of God and the literal second Elijah that would lead us into the new world. We anticipated fleeing into the desert at Mr. Armstrong's beckoning to await Jesus' return. Transgressions against any of the church's doctrines resulted in "disfellowshipping", similar to the Amish form of shunning where you were ordered not to come back to any church function and services, and all other baptized members were not allowed to speak to you at all. You in essence were "dead" to the church. This was a particular effective fear tactic because many of us had to leave our families and friends because we weren't allowed to associate with anyone who continually talked bad about our church. The fear of isolation with the continued threat that if we left the church we lost our only chance of salvation with God kept me in line. All those years of believing false doctrines still affect me as I write this book. I wrestle with trying to let go of many false beliefs, but this church used incredibly strong fear tactics based on misquoted and distorted scriptural references. It will take time and patience which is something God has a lot of. This church was so radical in its beliefs about God and Jesus, that it alienated itself from traditional Christianity, and was considered a cult by traditional Christian sects.

Beware of "churches" that are very legalistic to the point of controlling every aspect of your life. Your relationship is with God and not a church affiliation. Satan will attempt to distort scriptures just enough so that from the outside it still sounds good.

Satan's Army:
Human Recruits
Now that I have mentioned some of the major players in the demon world I want to talk about modern satanic groups. There are four major categories of Satanists that exist today. Again this information comes from my past experience and

verbal indoctrination into Satanism.

Theist Satanists. This is the traditional Satan worshiping group. They worship Satan as an actual deity and employ the black mass in their ritual magic.

Leveyan Satanists. This group founded in the 1960's doesn't believe in an actual satanic entity, but believe in the dark force of nature. I once was associated with this group early on. They focus on all sorts of self-gratification as opposed to abstinences because to them being completely satisfied in the flesh means no frustrations. I remember a clever word play to remind myself of this concept: evil spelled backwards is live! Rather than trying to avoid the seven deadly sins, these Satanists indulge in them. They use satanic symbols mainly to instill fear on those regular people they feel deserve retaliation for any infraction committed against them. They are also big on the Black Mass.

Deistic Satanists. They believe in self-worship and that there is a supreme force of nature as opposed to an actual deity that governs our world and universe.

Duotheist Satanists. While this is considered a fringe group among true Satanists and is the object of their ridicule, it is gaining momentum within the rebellious youth movement. This group is Christian based in the fact that they believe that Satan isn't a god but a fallen angel who rebelled against God. They are convinced that Satan has a fighting chance to win against God in the next rebellion as depicted in Revelation. This is the group that teens trying to "get a rise" out of their parents will seek out just for the shock factor. It closely parallels Christianity because it wants verbal confrontations with Christians.

Rogue Satanists. While not an "official" category I am including it here because of all the groups, this is the most dangerous to themselves as well as to others. "Rogue" comprises of an individual or small band of individuals who interpret Satanism to fit their needs. Some (like I did) devote energy to conjuring up entities without full knowledge of its implications.

Some have no codes of conduct or belief system other than bringing mayhem to anyone they feel deserve it. They make it up as they go with a strong tendency to hurt and maim people and animals. In the other categories of Satanism animal sacrifice is not done. Many (but not all) in this group get their kicks out of setting cats on fire or gutting a dog alive. They wear their Satanism on their sleeve literally, proudly displaying satanic images on their clothing. Demons particularly enjoy flocking to these easily influenced "rogue" individuals. People, especially young adults who have been pushed to the brink by bullying will often start with this brand of Satanism to retaliate against their attackers because it doesn't require any initiation or affliation.

One way that you can ascertain if someone you know is a true Satanist is to refer to them as a devil worshipper. True Satanists abhor this term and find it very offensive. They equate "devil worshiper" with someone referring to an African American using the "N" word. If you call someone a devil worshiper and they bristle over that title, it may be an indication that they are a Satanist, or at the very least have knowledge over why such a term is considered derogatory. It isn't conclusive proof, but it may confirm your suspicions that there is true satanic involvement at some level. Also if you ever heard mention of these organizations; Church of Azazel, Order of the Eternal darkness, and Temple of Diabolic Youth, they are the main true devil worshiping organizations today that worship Satan as a deity. They would only be known to those individuals who have explored true satanic worshiping groups.

Witches and Warlocks

I want to mention that witches aren't Satanists. They don't worship the god Baphomet like devil worshipers do. Great confusion surrounds this fact because many groups of witches believe in the Celtic horned god "Cernunnos" also going by the Greek name of "Pan" who is half man and half horned beast. Witches have been accused of devil worship all throughout the dark ages and demonized during the Salem witch trials back in the 1600's. While there are differences between the two groups, both reject God, Jesus, and all forms of Christianity. Even though witches claim not to enlist the aid of demons, they do so unknowingly thereby putting their souls at an equal risk as that of a Satanist. Witches use a pentagram which is a five pointed star contained within a circle. Satanists also utilize the pentagram but invert it so that the upside down star resembles horns.

Witches practice "magick" and not magic. Magic is what a magician performs in front of an audience like pulling a rabbit out of a top hat. Practicing magick incorporates rituals, incantations, invocations, spells, and curses. Being closely linked to earth energies, most witches base their practice on the moon phases of full moon and dark moons. Dark moons are nights where there is not even a sliver of moon. This is when the dark powers are at their greatest. Full moons are times when lunar influences are at their peak and have the most powerful effect on incantations. Those who practice witchcraft will call upon "energies" to help them. Witches are confident that these energies are spirits of the universe. In reality they are calling on demons who have disguised themselves as spirits of the universe. These fallen angels are quick to respond to any calls sent out by anyone through any means seeking some sort of cosmic spiritual illumination. Witches are fair game and an open invitation for demonic manipulation.

Wicca is a type of pagan belief where the initiated are called witches. Wiccans are nature based with a great goddess as the principle deity. Their motto of "harm none", is most commonly seen on car bumper stickers today. All Wiccans are witches, but not all witches are practitioners of Wicca, nor are all pagans witches. There are many forms of witchcraft out there besides Wicca. Dark art witches and warlocks are people who use magic to get whatever they want. They won't think twice about causing harm to anyone who gets in their way. This group will call on evil spirits or "dark energies" (as they refer to them) to inflict harm on another who have crossed them in any manner.

All one has to do to create a personalized brand of witchcraft is to self-study a particular form of witchcraft, then exalt themself to a high priestess or priest, adapt practices to fit their goals, and look for recruits (also called an "owan" which means uninitiated one) to develop a coven. A coven is a group of 12 witches under the leadership of a high priestess which brings the coven number up to 13.

Most witches like the Wiccans however believe in a mother goddess concept of some form. It is more of a pagan religion as opposed to a demon worshiping religion. Only a woman can be called a witch. Men who practice witchcraft are known as warlocks. That isn't to say that there aren't dark art witches or warlocks out there that conjure and set demons on others, but generally most witches and warlocks are unfairly lumped into the Satanist group due to the past hysteria, misconceptions, and persecutions of them during the Middle Ages. That doesn't mean dabbling in witchcraft is any less dangerous!! It doesn't matter if you get run over by a bus traveling at 55mph, or a compact car traveling at the same rate of speed; both will make you just as equally dead. Apply this same analogy when comparing the dangers of practicing witchcraft over Satanism.

Terminology Used with Satanists and Witches

I am including a list of the common words and phrases used in both groups so as to familiarize you with the terminology associated with witchcraft and Satanism.

Esbats – derived from the old French meaning to "frolic and amuse oneself". It is the religious ceremonial gathering of a witches' coven.

Invocation – the ritual to summon up a deity (witchcraft) or demon (Satanism). Best performed on certain nights at abandoned places, sites of tragedy, or in cemeteries.

Incantation – the "prayer" spoken to invoke a particular demon or deity. The incantation must be spoken exactly as it is written at a specific time otherwise nothing will happen.

Professio – this is the pact made with a demon which spells out all the terms proposed by the demon and must be signed with the person's own blood.

Grimoires – also known as "the book of shadows". It is a collection of written spells by witches contained in a black bound book.

Le Messe Noir – or Black Mass of Satanism. This is the

blasphemous ceremony that mocks the Catholic Mass. It includes a complete parody of the Eucharist celebration.

Ritual magick – is the performance of a formal ceremony held at a certain place set aside for such purposes.

Lesser magick – it is manipulative magic consisting of spells, charms, and curses and is mainly performed outside of ceremonial magic.

Spell casting – a declaration of intent put into specific words and in a concrete statements. In casting spells the idea is to bend the probabilities of success in your favor by calling on help from inhuman entities. There is a very specific want and outcome by the one who casts the spell.

Inhuman entity – a spirit that was never incarnated into human form. Low level inhuman entity is another term for a demon. It is used increasingly more by ghost hunters because it sounds less frightening than the term "demon".

Curse – a curse is a very potent spell designed to harm someone else physically, mentally, emotionally, or all three combined.

Chapter 5

The Nature of a Demon

Simply put, demons are 100% evil. When demons rebelled against God they rejected all things holy. Unlike humans, demons don't have a conscience so they aren't conflicted over good versus evil in thought or action. Lacking a conscience they are incapable of remorse which means they have no regret over their participation in the rebellion that led to their fall from heaven. Angels, when first created, were "programmed" (it's the closest word I could find that gets the point across without causing a theological debate) to carry out God's will. At the moment a third of the angels decided to rebel against God, their "programming" switched from serving God to serving Satan. Their angelic desire to serve and worship God corrupted into an insatiable hunger to annihilate all forms of Godliness and to exalt themselves as gods. Whereas before, (that is, in the beginning) they were filled with complete and total love for God, the fallen angels then became consumed by nothing but 100% hatred for their

Creator and all His creation.

Like a man–eating great white shark that exists entirely by instinct, demons are programmed to ruin INSTINCTIVELY all the Godliness in this world. When sharks sense splashing in the water it is instinct that draws them in because they have been programmed to correlate splashing with a fish in distress. A shark doesn't "reason" whether the splashing is the result of a distressed seal or a human swimming by. Created without a conscience, sharks attack without the slightest bit of remorse because that is all they know how do to; it's their nature. Apply this same principle to demons. Without a conscience they function solely on evil instinct. Even though demons have a keen intellect, you can't reason with a demon. Their ravenous lust for revenge from being expelled from heaven dominates their existence. A demon's "programming" of total destruction of all goodness leaves them incapable of mercy, compassion, and being honest and truthful. I have 47 years of experience dealing with the demonic first hand so what I just described has been accurate in my experiences with them.

By siding with Satan the fallen angels became infused with pride. Pride led to a spirit of disobedience which defined their character forever. This spirit of disobedience doesn't allow for harmonious cooperation among demons so they are prone to infighting and bickering amongst themselves. Despite this pettiness however, demons are united in their goal to destroy as many human souls as they can. In spite of their differences, all demons have one goal in common: to carry out Satan's diabolic plan to deceive mankind into rejecting God. For example, when we feel wronged by another person it can tap into unresolved suppressed anger locked deep inside of our soul. Anger justifies feelings of hurt by hurling hostile words at those who wronged us.

Anger erects barriers that shut out anything holy while at the same time lowering our defenses against demonic influences. Anger is like blood in shark infested waters. Even trace amounts attract these vicious creatures from quite a distance. Just as sharks come in closer to investigate this "scent", so do demons. Resentment, hurt, and anger invite other tormentors in. Demons are pack hunters! In Luke 11:26 we see demonic cooperation when it comes to the ruin of a soul, "Then it [demon] goes and takes seven other spirits more wicked than itself, and they go and live there [in a person]."

A demon's nature is to lie. Jesus in John 8:44 (NIV) calls Satan the father of lies, "He was a murderer from the beginning, not holding to the truth, for there is no truth in him. When he lies he speaks his native language, for he is a liar and the father of lies." Demons are masters of deception. The problem with compromising or striking a bargain with a liar is the fact that you can't trust them to follow through with their end of the deal. Demonic strategy is one of pure deception and inversion of Godly principles where good is evil and evil is good. 1 John 5:19 says that the whole world lies under the influence of Satan. For example in our society today, abortion is commonly accepted as part of a "reproductive health" procedure as opposed to be seen for what it really is; the killing of an innocent unborn child. Devout Christians who don't compromise on Godly principles are viewed as "fanatical" as opposed to upholding righteousness at all costs. Wrong is becoming right, and right is becoming wrong.

Accept the fact that there is no place on earth where you can hide from Satan and his demons. For now the entire world is their domain. Demons are everywhere and all around us. Demons are spirit and not bound by our physical laws which means they can travel anywhere at will in the flash of a second. Their evil has blended into our reality on so many levels that we are no longer aware of it so we accept it as just part of the natural order of things. For instance, the outright animal cruelty documented by various animal welfare groups in factory farms that produce our eggs hasn't sparked a mass protest by consumers. Many people just refuse to think about that part of it. What about the corruption in politics, or the starvation and ethnic cleansing occurring in third world countries? Why has a video game called "Grand Theft Auto" where the object of the game is not getting caught stealing a car become a favorite among our teens? The further away from God we drift, the easier it becomes to embrace the lie that evil is a normal and an unchangeable part of our world.

The Roles Within the Demonic Hierarchy

Since the fallen angels were part of the celestial hierarchy they still maintain their particular "rank". The structure of hell mirrors the celestial hierarchy as a polar opposite. Demonic responsibilities correspond with the celestial duties they once had but now they carry out these duties for evil and not good. It is impossible to positively identify how many fallen angels defected from each specific triad. Since each angel rank was created by God for specific duties, generally angels don't carry out the duties of other ranks in the other triads. The same principle applies to the fallen angels.

Since Satan as former Cherubim has declared himself as the ultimate authority ruling over demons, I am confident he ranks the highest. I don't believe any Seraphim rebelled otherwise they would have authority over Satan. As a Cherub he was in the first triad that surrounded the throne of God. He was part of God's inner circle and his duties were designed to reflect that status. Satan's Cherubim "programmed" duties didn't change with his fall. Instead it became perverted. That means Satan's main focus and thrust of his wrath today is directed at striking as close to God as he possibly can in this world. Satan knows the church is as close to God as he can get. His "personal" mission is to destroy her from every angle including from within through scandal, infiltration of the clergy, controversy, bad press, and financial woes.

It is an established fact in the world of Satanism that Satan doesn't make house calls. As a former Cherub he isn't designed to interact with humans like you or me on a regular basis. His interest focuses on matters directly relating to God. That being said, there are exceptions as seen in the bible. Satan will directly attack individuals who have a special connection and mission from God. Holy people such as the prophets, Jesus and His apostles, and some Saints whom God personally chose to carry out specific Godly directives affecting the Church or the entire membership of the Body of Christ attracts Satan's personal intervention.

Even though Satan himself doesn't personally intervene in the affairs of mere mortals, he arrogantly claims credit for doing so. Think of Satan as the master mind terrorist who orders his minions to carry out his instruction for the ruin of souls. Osama Bin Laden, the master mind behind the twin towers tragedy didn't personally attack the towers but is the one credited for its destruction. Bin Laden received credit for many of his planned terrorist attacks around the world even though he never left his hidden headquarters and never fought on the front lines. Demons are hell's terrorists who in the name and authority of Satan carry out his mission to destroy souls. Satan takes the credit for it. So in I Peter 5:8 when it says, "be sober and vigilant for Satan walks about like a roaring lion searching for someone to devour", this admonition reflects on all demonic spirits in the service of, and name of Satan.

Upper Level Demons and Lesser Demons

The higher ranked fallen angels are more primarily concerned with the ruin of cities, nations, and countries. Their rank is higher than that of an archangel or angel so in hell they hold the titles of princes, ministers, grand dukes, and ambassadors. Archangels and angels concern themselves mainly with human affairs so those in this triad that rebelled are the demons that we must contend with on a daily basis. Fallen archangels are referred to as upper level demons. Generally these more powerful demons will only manifest in someone's life as the result of that person's deliberate or inadvertent summoning or invoking of their presence. On rare occasions, a person steeped in the black arts can conjure up such a demon to torment a targeted otherwise innocent individual. It doesn't happen very often because of the consequences of such an act. The universal law of black magic warns that what you conjure up and set on someone will come back on you.

When making a pact with Satan, the terms of the pact are drawn up by an upper level demon summoned up by the person wanting to strike the deal. As a former archangel, upper level demons still retain their former "job description" as messengers. Once the blood pact is signed, the upper level demon carries this signed message back to hell. When it comes time for hell to collect on the bargain, these same demons deliver collection notices to the parties involved. Upper level demons are particularly nasty, powerful, and have greater abilities to manipulate the physical environment surrounding an individual than just a common garden variety demon. They can throw a human across a room, kill or maim animals and pets, and give super human strength to the person they possess. All interactions with them are especially frightening and dangerous. Upper level demons go to great lengths to conceal their identity and are very reluctant to give their name. Unless specifically conjured up during a satanic ritual they prefer to remain anonymous. Unlike lower level demons, they won't brag about their name and rank. Instead, in harassing the person they will attempt to get that individual to believe that they are going insane. Jesus says in the Gospel of Luke that demons are continually seeking rest. They find this rest by attaching themselves to us, and in worse case (extremely rare) scenarios, by possession. To be identified means they risk being cast out and forced to wander in search of a new "home". Something they aren't keen on doing.

Fallen angels are known as lower level or lesser demons. These are the demons who are constantly on the prowl looking for their next human target and the ones you and I must be on guard against. Being referred to as a "lower level" demon doesn't make them any less dangerous! Demons want to be worshiped by us because when we worship a demon it appeals to their prideful nature. To worship means to exalt which is exactly what they crave. Demons feel they have nothing to lose and everything to gain by destroying a soul. Their mentality is like that of a company CEO arrested for corporate crimes who says, "Well if I am going down I will take as many with me as I can".

Demons are individual spirits with distinct personalities. Some want to be identified by name such as Aguares, Lilith, or Samael. Others prefer to be identified by their chief specialty such as the "spirit [demon] of infirmity" in Luke 13:10. It is important to remember an important distinction when it comes to demonic specialties. A demon who proclaims that he is the demon of infirmity doesn't imply that all illnesses are demonically linked. It simply means that it is his chief method of operating in susceptible individuals. The same applies to demons of fear, anger, lust, etc. Being afraid or getting angry doesn't automatically mean that you are possessed by a demon of fear or anger. Coming down with a terrible illness such as colon cancer more than likely is due more to family genetics, age, or lifestyle than a specific demon. While it may be a demonic temptation to get you to react in anger, a demon can't force you to become angry. Demons cannot control your emotions or thoughts! That decision is yours alone.

No One is Compelled to Evil — We Choose It

Even little children can decide to choose evil. To pretend we are never attracted to evil is like pretending evil doesn't exist. I have seen my share of toddlers get into a "fist–i–cuff" over a favorite toy. Getting upset over a playmate's not wanting to share a coveted toy is an emotion and not an act of evil, but deliberately hauling off and slapping the other toddler is. It was a deliberate choice to inflict pain on the other child. No matter how badly someone mistreats you, retaliation doesn't happen without full awareness on your part that it is a deliberate choice to commit a wrong doing. For that matter, forgiveness is also a deliberate choice. It can stop an argument dead in its tracks, yet most of the time we choose to continue the argument now infused with fresh hurtful and spiteful words. Why is it so much easier to give in to evil? Because we have become erroneously programmed by the demons themselves into believing that sinning is a way of life and unavoidable by the demons themselves! No one is immune from sin, yet no one is forced to sin either. God gives each one of us a choice to choose good or evil. It is called free will. It is a universal law that even the demons must abide by. Demons need your permission before they can take up residence in your head. All too freely do we carelessly and unknowingly hand over our free will to them.

Because of free will demons can't invade your space unless you invite them in. Free will means you alone must decide to choose good or evil. Free will is neither evil nor good, but is neutral. No one, not a demon, or God can force you to make that decision because God will not go against Himself. Demons will however use coercion to falsely convince you that you don't have a choice. You always have the power to say "no" to evil. Demons can manipulate and influence people around you as a way to gain entrance into your life. It is only when you allow an individual or a situation to dictate how you feel and react that you open yourself up to unwanted negative demonic energies. Evil loves free will because humans particularly when emotionally charged will tend to follow their heart (emotions) instead of thinking rationally. Demons will take advantage of the human tendency to react emotionally instead of rationally. Crimes of passion most often manifest demonic thought tampering.

Cemeteries are Like Vacation Homes for Demons

Despite popular belief, ghosts do not inhabit or wander around cemeteries. In the gospels of both Matthew and Mark, a demon possessed man runs out of the tombs to meet Jesus in the region of Gerasenes. Tombs are synonymous with cemeteries. Drawn in by emotions of pain and loss, demons frequent cemeteries feeding on the residual traces of negative energies such as grief left behind by grieving mourners. Death, loss, and overwhelming hopelessness incite a feeding frenzy. Their hunger for these feelings is insatiable; like locusts they flock from cemetery to cemetery in search of their next "meal". Demons aren't permanent residents of a specific place and they do not pose an immediate threat to the funeral attendees or loved ones visiting the gravesites of the dearly departed. No one ever dies alone. No one ever grieves the loss of someone they loved and cared for alone either. At the wake, the funeral Mass, and graveside, every mourner's guardian angel stands united together to create a circle of protection around the entire funeral party. We may be so grief stricken that we cannot feel God's presence in our life in that moment. Rest assured that the entire family of God is in fact present in that very moment keeping vigil over us. Where God is, demons aren't, so it is safe to go to the cemetery for a funeral. It is also safe to visit the graveside of a loved one.

It is equally safe to visit cemeteries for historical and genealogical purposes as long as you aren't in a negative frame of mind. Emotional distress of any sort acts as a GPS locator pinpointing your location to nearby or passing through demonic spirits seeking out negativity especially in cemeteries. Teenagers are most at risk when they decide to tempt fate with scary pranks and "dares" taking place in a cemetery. Teens tend to be emotionally conflicted during adolescence, and this negative energy when combined with any occult curiosity acts as a handshake welcoming in all demonic spirits drawn in by their teenage curiosity of the macabre.

The quickest way a demon gains entrance is through occult involvement of any type. It doesn't matter whether you practice black magic or just go to the latest 3–D horror movie; both are an open invitation to demons that they won't refuse. It's not the horror flick itself that opens the door to demonic influences. It is the state of mind these movies create. Many people who see such movies can't help but mentally reflect on the concepts and content long after the movie ended. Some become more curious of the occult and some others will develop fears. Either way focusing on scary scenes or pondering the portrayal of evil sends out a signal to the spirit realm that your mind is now receptive to negative influences. No need to attach a RSVP with your invitation either because the arrival time of evil entities will almost be instantaneous. Even the smallest hole in the bottom of a boat will over time cause the boat to fill up with water and sink if not dealt with. The same applies to occult involvement. There is no "safe" or "neutral" zone that allows for experimentation without consequences. Involvement of any kind no matter how insignificant opens the door to the spirit realm no matter how harmless it appears on the surface. When you open your mind to the spirit world you can't regulate what comes through. I can't stress this enough: demons cannot invade your space unless invited in by you.

Feelings of being "drawn" to a cemetery that hold no personal connection can be an early indicator of demonic probing. Especially, if once in the cemetery someone is overcome with feelings of doom and gloom. On sensing someone in a cemetery in emotional distress, demons will often attempt to attach themselves to that person and follow them home. This poses a big problem for the mourner in the cemetery who no longer believes in God or denies His existence all together. A person's obstinate refusal to believe in God acts as a big bright neon sign flashing above their head spelling out, "Free admission for demons today!"

It is natural during an experience of death to grieve and feel overwhelming loss whether you believe in God or not. Getting through the days and weeks that follow on auto-pilot with a feeling of numbness is all part of the grieving process. Without a belief system however, there is no hope of a future reuniting with the one lost. This is the point in the life of the bereaved when they are so vulnerable their defenses are almost nonexistent. That black dismal void of permanent loss allows for demonic suggestion to influence the non believer's behavior. It is unnatural and demonically induced while in grief to become self-destructive via substances, addictions, or reckless behavior. Some will blame God for unfairly taking their loved one away from them. This resentment is enough to attract the evil ones into the personal space of a grief–stricken person where the demons then can manipulate that grief into self-destructive behaviors. Demons do this by siding and agreeing with feelings of unfairness. They whisper into the unsuspecting person's subconscious, "Yes, God is so unfair to rob you of your loved one while He allows a wicked person to live," or, "How can God be a loving God to have allowed someone to suffer in such miserable agony during a terminal illness?" or, "Only a cruel God would allow your child to die. It's OK to hate God."

During the grieving process there is hardly any clarity as to how death is part of some master plan for our growth. Having lost someone I dearly loved I knew all the rational Christian explanations of why death is unavoidable. I also have faith that one day when I get to heaven I will see this person again. Still, while consumed with grief it is difficult to not feel the pain of permanent absence of a loved one in your life. Without faith and hope it is all too easy during this time to become resentful of God. Any negative emotion directed at God is sweet perfume to a demon who will capitalize on this opportunity and attach themselves to the bereaved person.

Turning Your Back on Evil Doesn't Discourage Demons; It Only Infuriates them Even More

In a world flooded with the influences of evil it takes deep commitment to resist evil and follow God in God's plan. Many will fall by the wayside as Jesus illustrated in his parable about the sower. For each of you who commit whole heartedly to follow God, the Holy Spirit comes to dwell in your heart. You send out a loud and clear message to the demons that you belong to God and that God is more powerful than Satan. This enrages them because evil can't exist in goodness. Demons arrogantly believe that they are the rulers over the earth; they are everywhere and around everyone. The entire world and every human being is their "space". As the Holy Spirit dwells in you, it permeates all around your space where demons lurk. The Holy Spirit evicts the evil ones and their evil temptations out from this space.

Feeling crowded out of their perceived rightful living space they are consumed by retaliation and revenge. It becomes personal to them when you hand them an eviction notice. Demons are addicted to instant gratification. Like a heroin addict desperately craving a fix that mugs or robs the nearest person they think has money on them, demons craving retaliation impulsively attack anyone around you. It could be a family member or the bag boy at the grocery store. Knowing that someone strong in the faith can't be easily influenced, the evil ones invade the space of those around you not so strong. Picking up on a weakness or unconfessed sin which allows them access to manipulate someone's thoughts, they begin to influence this person's thoughts with negativity towards you. It is a "two for one" special. They attack you by influencing someone else to do their bidding against you. Even someone close to you or who you trust can be vulnerable to a secondary attack by demons. Perhaps those in your life who appear to be very faithful may have some hidden spiritual issue(s) you aren't privy to. Trust me; the demons are aware of this person's inner struggle. No one is immune from this type of demonic manipulation.

Demonic Tactics

Paul in 2 Corinthians 2:11, states that we are unaware of the Evil One's schemes against us. Demons will use others to knock you off balance just to get you to question and doubt your faith. Demons can be subtle, sneaky, cunning, and persistent!! They can negatively impact any material attachments such as personal finances and worldly possessions. Their biggest thrill comes from catching someone unaware and blindsiding them. Demons use temptations, distractions, accusations, and half truths to seduce you away from Godliness. They can appear to you in dreams either literally or disguised as someone or something else. Remember demons are pure spirit and as such don't have a particular shape. They can visually manifest themselves into your worst frightening image, be it a horned cloven hoofed creature with bat wings, or a clown.

Generally though, a demon that infests a person or household will remain invisible for the duration of the stay and while it torments the occupant(s). They can create smells of sulfur, rotting flesh, and other putrid smells to enhance your fear of them. At times they can strike you with a non life–threatening sickness where there seems to be no medically explained cause for it. Just look at Job or the woman afflicted with an illness for eighteen years that our Savior healed in Luke 13:11–16; Jesus referred to her as, "a daughter of Abraham whom Satan has bound".

But by far, the quickest way you grant demons free access into your head is by not rebuking temptations. They are masters at wearing down your resolve to resist an evil enticement. The five senses are the gateways into our every earthly desire. Demons are experts in detecting all of our unspoken and hidden vices and carnal appetites. They will try to enter through the five senses in order to gain access to your thoughts. By manipulating circumstances that enhance the sensitivity of the sense they are targeting, demons will use seduction that appeals to that particular sense.

For instance let's say that "Fred" has a weakness for pornography. He decides to give up the depravity by throwing away all videos, magazines, and related items. He attends church every week. His mind is filled with a deep conviction to purge himself from all such impure thoughts. There is no way a demon can penetrate through that sort of mental barrier. So the demon probes for weaknesses in his commitment by setting a trap for the physical senses. Fred gets on a plane and the in–flight movie contains numerous steamy intimate love scenes. This visual temptation is achieved through the sense of sight. Just like in a game of poker, the demon studies Fred's face looking for any tell tale non–verbal signs of how he will react to the "cards on the table" (in this case, the movie).

The mind and body must be one united front standing firm against demonic assaults. We can mentally convince ourselves that we are able to resist our evil urges, but that isn't enough. We must also resist the lure of the physical sensations of touch, sight, smell, taste, and sound that can overpower our mental resolve of abstinence. How Fred handles this temptation determines how the demon will respond next. I will say this so many times that you will get sick of hearing it; demons CANNOT force you to do anything! The choice is yours alone!

If Fred doesn't rebuke this temptation by choosing to read a magazine or look out the window instead of up at the movie screen, then he relinquished his free will. His mind and body wasn't unified in his commitment to resist temptation. The demon on seeing Fred glance repeatedly up at the screen during love scenes knows he has breached Fred's impenetrable mental fortress. The evil one now has entered through the gateway of the senses and roams without restraint in Fred's reasoning capabilities. Stronger visual temptations will follow in rather rapid succession. The demon now in a position of influence will short circuit Fred's reasoning abilities. The demon will falsely convince Fred that he might as well indulge in his pornographic cravings at that moment because Fred knows he is going to cave into them anyway; it's only a matter of time.

Don't Attempt to Go at it Alone

Demons are everywhere and all around us, but so are the Holy Angels. God knows how cunning Satan and his cohorts are and doesn't expect us to be victorious against them on our own. At the first sign of temptation cry out to the Blessed Mother to send her angels to help fight your demonic tormentors. Cry out to Jesus and rebuke the temptation in Jesus' name. Don't forget that your guardian angel is around you every minute of the day ready to assist you in these struggles. Be sure to ask for the heavenly angel's help otherwise they are compelled to stand back and honor the person's free will. They too need to be invited in. I want to leave you with an admonition to resist temptation taken from the book of James chapter 1:12–15 (NIV):

> "Blessed is the man who perseveres under trial, because
> when he has stood the test, he will receive the crown

of life that God has promised to those who love him. When tempted no one should say, 'God is tempting me'. For God cannot be tempted by evil, nor does he tempt anyone; but each one is tempted when, by his own evil desire, he is dragged away and enticed. Then after desire has conceived, it gives birth to sin; and sin, when it is full grown gives birth to death."

Chapter 6

The Biggest Secret Demons Don't Want Revealed

Legions of demons prowling the earth lie in wait for us. Demons view us as inferior weak vermin who don't stand a chance against all their wiles. Demonic spirits are very smug in their belief that they can influence us without us being aware of their presence. Demons, having such a high opinion of themselves, will at times on a whim spontaneously attack you because they know they can. Seizing on a sudden opportunity where they feel you are vulnerable because of what you are thinking at the moment, they may not always formulate a battle plan before acting. They will make it up as they go. These impulsive "hits" aren't as well fortified as a complex targeted strategic attack. Don't get me wrong, demons tend to be very calculating, and **all** attacks can be dangerous. It is just that they can't resist passing up on any unexpected openings you may unintentionally create. I have personally witnessed these types of attacks on myself and others around me so many times I lost count. They probe for our every weakness and utilize all the knowledge gained through their torment of human beings throughout the ages. Being the ultimate egotists, demons are convinced they won't and can't fail in getting you to falter and sin every time. Unfortunately, man's history supports their conceitedness. This over confidence makes for a very aggressive enemy who will at times rashly come charging headlong at you out of thin air. Their underestimation of us can be used to our advantage, especially when we are assaulted by an impulsive hit.

Can Demons Read My Mind?

I want to make it clear that demons cannot read minds. They can't access your memory to view what you did last week, last month, or last year. Demons **can** however read active thoughts. Bear with me as I try to put this complex concept into simple terms. Active thought means what you are thinking about in the moment. It's the conversation you are having with yourself in your head. For example, as I type this page I am also simultaneously actively thinking (or having a conversation in my head) over whether this concept I am proposing will make sense to you or not. Being "deep in thought" is another form of active thought because at that moment in time you are concentrating many thoughts on a particular subject.

The act of "thinking" generates electrical impulses between your neural pathways in the brain. Electrical brain impulses are a form of energy. If all your thoughts and memories were to congeal into a solid mass, it would quickly clog up the limited room in your skull. Think of your thoughts as wood burning in a campfire. A roaring flame puts out a lot of energy and is very intense. Eventually, as the wood burns it emits a grayish blue smoke as it begins to disintegrate into ash, leaving more room to add fresh wood (new thoughts). You don't have to stand over the campfire to know it is burning. You can see the smoke rise from a distance, and it is the smoke that alerts you that the wood is burning. A roaring campfire generally is an inviting sight as we sit alongside the fire pit mesmerized by the orange hue of the flames. The grayish blue smoke is a positive sign beckoning your camp buddies to gather around the campfire for a marshmallow roast. However, if you were to throw petroleum based trash in the campfire, the oil would billow out a black menacing carcinogenic cloud of smoke. Even just one plastic bread bag would generate a noticeable amount of pitch black smoke. Let's face it, midnight black smoke isn't an inviting sight for a positive experience. Who would want to toast a marshmallow over such a fire, especially when the park rangers specifically instructed each camper against such an unethical and dangerous practice?

Many of our thoughts that we intently focus on, good or bad, are like a campfire. When our "campfire wood" (our mental focal point) focuses on only goodness and Godliness, the grayish "smoke" it produces, "invites" all holy beings to gather with and around you to enjoy the warmth of the fire. If instead you carelessly or willfully toss some plastic refuse into the fire (a negative thought), the black billowing smoke sends out a signal to those familiar with unscrupulous burning procedures. I doubt happy campers would gather around your smoking black fire. Those who would be attracted would be hooligans who enjoy participating in such deceitful methods; in this case demons. Positive thinking draws in goodness, but negative thoughts (like black billowing smoke) draws in negativity which is an aphrodisiac to demons.

We may devote a lot of energy to a thought(s) but most thoughts sort of "dissipate" like "smoke" from a campfire over time. Generally speaking most people don't have the ability for total recall of every thought they conceived in their lifetime. Do you even remember what the main focus of your thoughts were for the day last Friday? Where did those thoughts you can't remember go? Important thoughts will be stored in memory and remain there as energy and not as a physical mass. Without the ability to read minds, demons can only perceive what is going on in your head by picking up on current thoughts. So, if in the moment you are having a negative thought and a demon is nearby, it will be attracted to this negativity because negativity is familiar to them; it appeals to their essence of evil.

God's Law of Universal Attraction

God created a universal cosmic law of attraction where like attracts like. This universal law manifests all around us on a daily basis. You can read about it more in a physics book. Horses are attracted to and herd together with other horses and not chickens. Likeminded people form friendships and groups. Like attracts like. For instance, how many professing Christian teens would join a violent street gang? None, because there would be a complete opposite belief system between the gang members and the devout Christian. People with cheery personalities who laugh a lot tend to draw more people to them than say someone who is sullen and depressed all the time. We are attracted to things, places, and people on a physical level that share things in common with us.

You emit an energy field without even being conscious of it. Your body tends to reflect high energy levels nonverbally through body posture, facial gestures, and movements.

Think about the last time you worshiped and praised God with all your heart in church. Your heart was filled with such joy, a smile graced your lips, and your thoughts were so filled with positive "energy" (love for God) that you telegraphed this high positive energy out to the world and those around you. Your thoughts were so positive that it attracted more of the same. For instance, someone saw your beaming smile during the service and then came up to you afterwards to say "hi" because they were attracted by the positivity you projected.

I am sure you may have wondered why there are times that God seems so much closer to you than at other times. Godly thoughts and contemplation sends out 100% pure love and the universal law of attraction also applies to the spirit realm, drawing closer all heavenly beings. In John 17:26 (NIV) Jesus in prayer to God the Father says, "I have made you known to them [the world], and will continue to make you known in order that the love you have for me may be in them and that I myself be in them."

If you focus your thoughts on Godly love, you will draw in all things holy because where there is love, there God is also. The purer the thoughts, the more you open yourself up to a deeper spiritual experience because holiness doesn't compete with ungodliness; holiness will not occupy the same space in your head with evil. During these positive moments, negative thoughts and energies can't permeate the barrier of holiness. In the law of attraction, evil and goodness are opposites and therefore aren't attracted to each other, but are instead repelled. Simply put; the more positive you are, the closer the connection is to God, shielding you from demonic intrusions.

Do Any and All Negative Thoughts Invite a Demonic Attack?

The answer is no. A negative thought will not automatically provoke an attack. It will however catch their attention. Physics 101 tells us that we human beings are electromagnetic power plants that generate all kinds of electrical impulses that govern everything our body does, be it brain waves or heartbeats. Over the last few years there have been scientific studies conducted to study our emotions. The overwhelming conclusion drawn from these careful experiments is that what we are feeling at any given moment causes vibrational energy waves to be emitted from our bodies.

Being mortal we don't have the same high level sensitivity as a spirit being does to pick up on these "waves", but we do manifest some ability. In today's lingo we call it "vibes". Say you came in to work one morning and saw Fred deeply engrossed in his paperwork. He is flicking his pen rather quickly in one hand, and doesn't even avert his gaze upwards when someone stops to ask him a question. A common expression a co–worker might say about him is, "Man, Fred is giving off a bad vibe this morning."

Fred's negative state of mind goes beyond body language. A lot of people just "sense" when someone is in a bad mood or even a happy mood for that matter. You can't just chalk it up to human nature when we tend to avoid people because of the "vibe" they are giving off. There is a growing body of scientific evidence correlating emotional energies and human interactions.

A thought is simply just a thought. A string of similar thoughts become an emotion. A pattern of repeated similar strings of thought turns into a mood. Emotions and moods cause physiological changes in the body through chemical neurotransmitters in the brain. The "energy" produced from these chemical reactions (both positive and negative) can be sensed by humans and spirit beings. Without turning this chapter into a quantum physics lesson, suffice it to say that the vibrational frequency emitted by us is likened to a spectrum. The lower end of the spectrum is negative comprising of fear, anger, hate, and the higher end is positive comprised of happiness, joy and love, with lots of variations and degrees pending on where you are on the spectrum. Our thoughts and emotions move up and down this spectrum based on our current state of mind.

Demons crave negative vibrations and actively seek them out. Any negative thought gives off a negative vibration that can draw them in. It doesn't mean you will be attacked, but for sure they are close. Demons "feed" (figuratively) on negative thoughts which in turn excite them. Once you produce one negative thought, it has a frequency level that easily connects with a demon because like attracts like. This gives the demon access to your thoughts where he will plant similar thoughts so as to stay in your space. Isn't it amazing how one negative thought "triggers" another and then another? If you have a negative thought that quickly snowballs into something much bigger, chances are you are tapping into demonically planted thoughts.

The Demon's Biggest Secret Weapon Used Against Us

The one thing a demon doesn't want you to ever find out is how they attempt to control your thoughts without your knowledge. They want us to consider every negative emotion and thoughts as "normal" and not part of their influence. This is their big secret because if we aren't aware of this tactic, then we won't put up any defenses against them. They don't want you to know this secret and have done a great job of manipulating psychology into explaining away the unexplainable as just part of the human psyche. One negative thought left unchecked will quickly spiral into a string of negative thoughts because demons attracted by the first thought, use that first thought as an opening to tamper with your thought processes.

Let's take for instance the negative thought of, "Mary hasn't called me in over a week; I wonder if she is mad at me." There is no evidence to support that thought, but still it leads to another similar thought, "Since she always calls me regularly, I know she must be mad." The next thought rapidly spirals down to, "What did I do to make her so mad at me?" There is no truth, only conjecture as to why Mary hasn't called, so what takes our mind down that slippery slope? It is demonic thought tampering (some people call it brainwashing). The demon infuses his negativity into the second thought hoping you won't analyze where that thought came from. If left unchecked, the demon begins to condition you into believing that these deceptive thoughts are absolute truth. As you begin to blame yourself for some imagined wrong you must have committed against Mary, that self-incrimination leads to unfounded guilt which quickly deteriorates into a negative self-image regarding the situation. The demon laughs at your not even recognizing that it is he and not you putting yourself through that misery.

The slightest bit of worry over anything be it being late for an appointment, or worrying over whether or not your blood tests will come back normal or not, will send out a "smoke signal" of negativity that demons respond to. Demons "feed" (figuratively) on everything that is negative. Getting angry at the lady who snuck into your parking space while you waited for a shopper to walk past provides critical "negative energy" for demons. Swearing at the guy who cut you off on the highway also provides critical "food" for a demon. All these negative thoughts or emotions are what demons can't get enough of, so they will do anything they can to keep more such feelings streaming out from you. Demons have an insatiable "hunger" for negativity.

An Aberrant Thought that Doesn't Seem to Fit the Situation Strongly Indicates Demonic Influencing is at Work!!!

If out of nowhere you get a strange negative thought that doesn't go with what you are focusing on, be sure it is a demonic "plant" to see if you will run with it. Demons are convinced that we are slaves to our own thoughts and emotions. For instance, I have just finished a phone conversation with my closest friend Sister Francanne. I feel happy and loved as I reflect on just how much joy she has brought into my life. All of a sudden I get this thought that contradicts how I am feeling. The thought goes, "This friendship won't last. She is 71 years old and will probably die within five years."

That is a demonic plant because it goes contrary to what I was feeling in the moment. Demons need to temper all vibrations of joy and happiness in order to bring it closer to their own vibration of negativity. They can't "work" in an environment of love and contentment because they aren't compatible with heavenly virtues. Just as you can't hook up the trailer bed of an 18 wheeler truck to a car, demons can't function alongside positive thoughts. They attempt to plant negative thoughts all the time, but the closer to God you are, the harder it is for them to succeed.

You need to understand that demons are all around us all the time. How close they come to you personally depends on you. You offer them entrance into your head by letting down your guard. Unconfessed sins, ambivalence towards attending church regularly, and harboring negativity of any sort, invite them into your personal space where they can attempt to access your thoughts. Remember demons have influenced and tormented mankind for eons making these fallen angels skilled in manipulating human behavior without our knowledge. They have learned to mimic human behavior without ever feeling it. Demons are only capable of total and absolute wickedness, which they inflict with brutal savagery any chance they get. By sowing a single seed of discouragement in the form of an aberrant thought, they attempt to make you feel utterly powerless and helpless over your emotions. The only way a demon can gain a foothold on your thoughts is if you react wrongly and give in to it!

Satan's Greatest Lie

The ability to manipulate our thoughts if given the chance without our awareness has allowed the greatest lie ever conceived appear as absolute truth in our head. This lie is simple but powerful: "My sins are too great for God to forgive me for them."

Have you ever sinned so badly that you wondered how God could forgive something like that? If you won't allow God to forgive you then you can't forgive yourself. You can't surprise or shock God with some sin no one has ever committed before. Self-condemnation is the worst punishment we tend to inflict upon ourselves unnecessarily. God is not the source of feeling unforgiveable. Feeling unforgiveable isn't a godly trait, but a demonic deception! It is being consumed by guilt and shame that leads many souls out of despair and hopelessness to resort to suicide because of this satanic lie. The plain truth is any sin will be forgiven if you are truly remorseful. If you don't believe me then believe Jesus. Jesus himself said in Mark 3:28 (KJV), "Verily I say unto you, all sins shall be forgiven unto the sons of man…". Romans 8:1 (KJV) reiterates this important truth, "There is therefore now no condemnation to them which are in Jesus Christ, who walk not after the flesh, but after the the Spirit."

The bible doesn't lie. God honestly and truly loves you! "Behold, what manner of love the Father has bestowed upon us, that we should be called the sons of God" (1 James 3:1, KJV).

Make no mistake about it; we are at war and there is never any fairness in warfare, particularly in spiritual warfare. Evil isn't fair. It doesn't matter anyway, as we don't need fairness. We need God's mercy. We can cry out to God for forgiveness and mercy and He will hear us because we are His sons and daughters. Ephesians 2:1–5 tells us,

> "As for you, you were dead in your transgressions and sins, in which you used to live when you followed the ways of the world and the ruler of the kingdom of the air, the spirit who is now at work in those who are disobedient. All of us lived among them at one time, gratifying the cravings of our sinful nature and following its desires and thoughts. Like the rest we were objects of wrath. But because of His great love for us, God who is rich in mercy, made us alive with Christ even when we were dead in transgressions–it is by grace you have been saved."

Mercy means compassion shown to an offender. No matter how hard you will try not to sin, there will be times when the evil ones deceive you into sinning. The plain truth is that you WILL offend God repeatedly in this lifetime. God knows that too, but it doesn't make Him love you any less. God is perfect love. God's mercy outlasts all of our wrong doings.

To add insult to injury demons sense our deepest temptations and weaknesses. They never forget how you have reacted to every temptation ever set before you. Like a rebellious teenager, a "no" means "yes" to them as they wait to hear, "I would never do that". I would never cheat on my wife. I would never molest someone. I would never abandon you. I would never embezzle money from my clients. I would never re–engage in my addiction of alcohol, drugs, gambling, or sex.

An "I would never" declaration sends out a challenge to demons closely associated with your particular weakness. They are attracted to the hint of arrogance attached to such a statement. Like a herd of charging cattle, they come running, clamoring for a chance to bind and hog tie you to your sin. They will bombard you with extremely strong mental and physical temptations. You can avoid putting out such a cattle call to the demonic herds grazing on human weaknesses by admitting you can't avoid it on your own. Saying instead, "I would never WITH GOD'S HELP cheat on my wife", shows humility. Humility is the exact opposite of pride. Humility repels demons. Even though you can be influenced by demonic thought tampering, know you can also be influenced by the Holy Spirit during any trial or temptation the evil ones throw at you. All you need to do is to cry out to Jesus for help. Rest assured He will dispatch all the angels required to help you fight off the temptation and/or negative thoughts. If you allow any aberrant thought to replace what the bible tells you is true—that is a demonic influence.

Using this Demonic Secret to Our Advantage

Pride blinds one from seeing the truth. This principle also applies to demons. The truth demons are unable to comprehend is described in James 4:7–8, "Submit yourselves then to God. Resist the devil and he will flee from you. Come near to God and he will come near to you."

James 4:7–8 is the key that unlocks the biggest secret demons don't want you to know. Contained within this powerful scripture is the ultimate weapon ready for deployment against the daily attempts of thought tampering we engage in with unseen demonic forces. It will blast a hole in the armor of secrecy surrounding the demon's most powerful plan of attack used against us.

Demons can't control human emotions; however, they try to manipulate the levels of emotion and tension in a room by planting negative thoughts. They will plant mental suggestions to increase negative energy (stress) in a room full of people. A stress reaction such as two people getting into an argument is an energetic reaction. Being drawn into an argument gives the demon exactly what he wants: your attention and energy. On top of that, the person around you who is angry and negative has not only attracted a demon but has come under its influence. Just being nearby is enough for you to feel the tug of the demon. This is what happens when a third person gets involved in a heated argument between two people. The common expression is, "He got caught up in the heat of the moment and got involved in the argument", but the reality is the close proximity to a demon had a negative effect on the third person who initially was a bystander. Philippians 4:6 (KJV) admonishes us not to give in to anxiety of any sort, "Do not be anxious about anything, but in everything, by prayer and petition, with thanksgiving, present your request to God." With "thanksgiving" means an attitude of gratitude (positive thoughts).

"Submit to God"

This is the critical first step. You have heard of the expression, "turn your life over to God". It isn't something you do once in your life and then go about your daily business like before. Fighting off any demon or demonic influences is serious stuff. Your soul is at stake! Submit to God by turning every day over to Him. That means when you awake in the morning, make it a declaration of intent to follow Godly principles. Say it out loud so that it becomes real to you. Demons can tamper with your thoughts but not your speech (except in cases of possession). By actually speaking the words, you are sending the demons a powerful message that you have unveiled their secret of thought tampering, and aren't going to be victimized by it any longer.

Free will or the ability to choose for ourselves what is right and wrong is our greatest strength, and at the same time our greatest weakness. Free will is a universal "law" decreed by God stating that all demons and heavenly hosts can't force a person to do good or evil. However, both sides are allowed to influence the individual to a certain extent. Demons will try to influence you to sin. Holy beings will encourage you to embrace Godly love. Free will teaches us that we have total responsibility for our actions. People wrongly assume that free will is a state of being and not a decision that is made over and over again each day whether they are aware of it or not. Free will allows us to grow spiritually because by understanding the ramifications of right and wrong, we deliberately choose right. Sadly, many people disregard the significance of this precious gift and carelessly make bad decisions without thinking through the ramifications which results in that choice ending badly. Then they blame everyone else including God for the consequences of their poor choice.

Take Fred for example. He is the fellow from chapter five with the pornography addiction. Fred's friend is getting married and he is invited to the bachelor party. Fred's other friend Jim advises him not to go because there is going to be a skimpily dressed girl that pops out of the cake, and Jim knows how badly Fred struggles with his addiction which is ruining his marriage. Fred willingly chooses to go anyway. The woman pops out of the cake not wearing much at all and all the guys at the party hoot and holler in excitement. Just seeing the woman triggers Fred's addiction and on the way home he chooses to commit adultery. Afterwards, the reality of having to face his wife after his act of infidelity bothers him. He blames his friend who is getting married for having a stripper in the first place. He blames his wife for not fulfilling all his physical desires "forcing" him to go outside of their marriage. He blames Jim for not being firmer in his resolve to stop him. Fred even blames God for not magically healing his addiction. All along it was Fred, not his wife, his friend Jim, or God, who exercised his right of free will to choose wrongly.

No demon, and not even a gun to your head has absolute power over you to force you to commit evil. Even the Saints who were martyred exercised free will by choosing to die rather than recant their faith in God. Yes, even at the point of death, when you feel there is no choice, the choice of how you die is yours alone. It is free will that dictates your action. You can choose to die embracing God's mercy for the one with the gun to your head, or you can choose evil and curse your murderer and his family.

Every time an aberrant thought pops in your head that you know is negative, immediately and verbally out loud affirm your intent of exercising your right to choose your free will to honor God and not Satan. There is no limit to how many times you can do this in a day, a week, or a year. When a demon attempts to push you in the wrong direction, push back for heaven's sake. Demons are just bullies who delight in intimidation. I will share a saying I thought up that I use as my mantra when I know a demon is trying to influence me to commit a sin; "When demons intimidate—don't imitate."

Follow St. Paul's example in Philippians 4:11–13 (NIV), "For I have learned to be content whatever the circumstances. I know what it is like to be in need, and I know what it is like to have plenty. I have learned the **secret** of being content in any and every situation, whether well fed or hungry, whether living in plenty or in want. **I can do everything through him who gives me strength.**"

How to Expose and Overpower Demonically Planted Thoughts;
"Resist the Devil and He Will Flee From You"

Never forget that demons "feed" on all negative thoughts and emotions. In 1 Corinthians 15:33 (KJV) we are admonished to, "Be not deceived; evil communications corrupt good manners." The best way to discourage them is to "starve them to death", or by "resisting the devil". Do this by:

1. Analyze any negative thought the moment it "pops" into your head. Ask yourself if you can substantiate the thought with facts. For example, you get stuck in traffic on your way to an important business meeting. As your anxiety level rises, your thoughts turn negative, "My boss is going to be really upset I missed the meeting." If you can verify that this will be a fact, then it isn't a demonic

plant. Acknowledge it is a true statement and pray to God for help when explaining why you were late to your boss. If however, the thought is, "My boss is going to kill me for missing this meeting", it more than likely is a demonic plant. Why? Because is there any truth that you will be murdered for being late? I know that the word "kill" is a commonly over used in expressions that we don't take seriously anymore. "I'm gonna kill him when I see him for forgetting my anniversary". "My mom's gonna kill me when she finds out". Satan is the father of lies and the expression itself is a lie, so who do you think is its author? God never lies. Being such a common expression that flows out of the mouth without even thinking about what it really means, allows the demon to influence your thoughts secretly, without your knowledge. If you still feel it is a harmless expression then I ask you this: would you say that expression to Jesus' face?

2. If you realize that the aberrant thought isn't factual, acknowledge it is a demonic plant. Once you acknowledge this, you "expose" the demon's attempt to infiltrate your thoughts. Their goal of planting negative thoughts is to get you to feel discouragement. Acknowledging being attacked allows you to reject the thought thereby disarming the demon and preventing further penetration into your thought processes. Exercise your free will. Consciously decide to reject the thought and ask for heaven's help in replacing the negative thought with a positive one. By doing this you are stripping the demon of his power and hold over your thoughts.

3. Change that thought at the first sign of discouragement. Replace it with another slightly more positive thought. Discouragement is born out of harboring and hanging on to a string of negative thoughts. By injecting a positive

thought, not only do you break the chain of negative thoughts, but it allows you to be receptive to heavenly help. Even just a single positive thought cracks the door open just enough for the Holy Spirit to begin to dispel the negativity that has overtaken you. "In the same way, the Holy Spirit helps us in our weakness. We do not know what we ought to pray for, but the Spirit himself intercedes for us with groans that words cannot express. And He who searches our hearts knows the mind of the Spirit, because the Holy Spirit intercedes for the saints in accordance with God's will", (Romans 8:26–27, NIV).

Replacing Negative Thoughts

When we are caught up in a trial, temptation, or discouragement, that is the critical time to replace any negative thinking with more positive thoughts. We are reminded not to let negative thoughts get the best of us in 2 Corinthians 4:8 (KJV), "We are troubled on every side, yet not distressed; we are perplexed, but not in despair". Again in 2 Corinthians 6: 4–10 Paul reminds us that even while in the depths of our sorrow we should strive to rejoice because we trust in the Lord. It is impossible to achieve a grandiose goal of being happy all the time, especially when you are under spiritual attack. The demon(s) are aiming to convince you that nothing will make you feel better than giving into temptations or wallowing in self-pity. They strive to convince you that you are all alone in this struggle deliberately so that you don't cry out for God. No one is ever alone when they need a heavenly angel the most. Still, it is you that must make the first move and ask your guardian angel to help fight off this attack every time!! There is no heavenly penalty incurred for over asking, but there is a demonic price to be paid for not asking at all. God will do His part if you do yours. You MUST grab onto a tiny morsel of hope, joy, or happiness. By doing that, it breaks the chain reaction created by a bunch of negative thoughts.

"Come Near to God and He Will Come Near to You"

At the first sign of negativity attempting to dominate your thoughts, immediately replace the negative thought(s) with a thought of goodness. You need to find a way to feel better when you or those around you are discouraged. Think of one small memory that brings you complete joy and reminds you of God. Maybe it's thinking about the day your child was born, or the beautiful sunset over the ocean you experienced on vacation, or holding a kitten for the first time. The key here is to actually "feel" that memory. Allow a "warm fuzzy" to overtake your mind and body in the moment. Why? By literally "feeling" the joy of the memory, it reconnects us with the love of God.

Love is a powerful emotion, especially pure Godly love, which when demons are exposed to it, causes them to flee writhing in pain. Love torments a demon!!! Love reminds us that we are children of God and not slaves of the devil. It is a satanic lie that God doesn't take a personal interest in you. He sends you His love in a way you can embrace; in a form that resonates personally to you. For me, I know God shows He loves me in a way I can understand. When I am undergoing a severe trial, or experiencing a melancholy I can't break free of, my otherwise aloof and unaffectionate cat snuggles in my lap purring up a storm. My cat who normally only acknowledges my existence at feeding times, makes me feel special and privileged by this action. Other times I will go out to do mundane evening barn chores and be witness to the most colorful, glorious sunset I have ever seen. God sends you His love daily. Be open to it. Look for it in the smallest of signs; be it a butterfly or an unexpected sudden memory of the happiest day in your life. Love is always a good choice, but you have to choose and look for it every day.

Do this every time you begin to feel negative or have a negative thought. Practice a "warm fuzzy" positive moment even when things are going well for you. As we consciously make this effort repeatedly, we will shift the balance of power back to God. Demons are trying to get you to believe that you are powerless over your circumstances. Turn this simple strategy into a daily habit. It won't be long before you will feel a closer connection to God by embracing His love that is manifested all around us. Your focusing on a moment of joy is a form of praise and worship to God. God WILL draw near to you!

Start small with maybe a minute or two every day to focus on one memory that brought you great joy. Smile; embrace the "feeling" of absolute love and gratitude for our Creator. Then work up to doing that two or three times every day until it becomes as normal as brushing your teeth. They say anything we do daily for thirty days becomes a habit, so turn this exercise into a habit. By doing so, it will become second nature, and not so difficult to employ in the moment when demons are infusing a negative thought. It will take effort at first because the demons will attempt to discourage this pattern because they don't want you to feel better. They will do this by injecting thoughts like, "This isn't going to work", or "I don't feel better even though I tried this exercise for a day", or "It is impossible to focus on even a second of joy when I feel so depressed, angry, or discouraged".

It will take time for this to feel "right" to you. After all, how many years have you been oppressed by demonic thought tampering? We have become accustomed to instant gratification or results in today's society. Not instantly feeling better after engaging in this exercise after just a couple of times, may trigger cynicism that it isn't going to work for you. If you feel that way, then analyze and realize where this thought is originating from. Don't fall back into your old pattern of accepting every negative thought as your own. Stop ignoring the source of your negative thoughts. Most of them will be lies to keep you from discovering that replacing negative thoughts with positive ones, beckons the holy angels to draw closer to you. It also enables the Holy Spirit to replace the lies in your head with truth. Jesus himself said in John 16:13, "But when he, the Spirit of truth comes, he will guide you into all truth."

Don't be afraid to ask God for help in combating these negative thoughts. He will listen and respond, if you just allow Him to. I will leave you with the assurance that this is an absolute fact! In Luke 11:9–13, Jesus himself gives you this assurance:

> "So I say to you: Ask and it will be given to you; seek and you shall find; knock and the door will be opened to you. For everyone who asks receives; he who seeks finds; and to him who knocks, the door will be opened. Which of your fathers, if your son asks for a fish, will give him a snake instead? Or if he asks for an egg, will give him a scorpion? If you then, though you are evil, know how to give good gifts to your children, how much more will your Father in heaven give the Holy Spirit to those who ask him?"

Chapter 7

*Demonic Weapons
of Mass Destruction*

Deceiving into not believing:
The Great Deception

Whereas the lesser demons prowl about the earth singling out potential victims to influence and torment, the higher up, upper level demons work on targeting the mass populace mainly by utilizing their expert skill of deception on a grand scale. Satan and his upper echelon demons have gone to great elaborate lengths to conceal their existence from people in general. Science, technology, psychology, self-enlightenment, and even Christianity all have been manipulated by Satan to shift the focus away from looking to God for answers, to looking to man or oneself for answers.

We are at the dawn of a terrible age where man replaces and becomes a "god" through the technology of cloning. The need to draw closer to God has been replaced with the need to be like, or play God. Isn't that how Lucifer started his rebellion and fall from heaven, by wanting to be like God? In Isaiah 14 Satan then still Lucifer said, "I will make myself like the most high".

How dare we compete against God with our 30 years or so of technological breakthroughs in the human genome, compared to His infinite eternal wisdom of perfect balance in creation. To artificially "create" life (man plays creator) through cloning, essentially is driven more for corporate monetary gains, without considering moral concerns and ethical ramifications. Satan is behind this ploy to write God out of the picture. By deceiving mankind into total and complete self-reliance, there will be no more dependence on God for answers to life's questions. Just like those early, now outdated and obsolete cell phones we carried (that were as big as an egg carton and weighed almost as much as a brick), Satan wants man to believe that God is an obsolete deity, invented by our primitive ancestors before the dawn of science.

This is the great deception: to get you to believe that there is no real spirit entity known as the "devil"; only a force of good and evil inherent within us all since birth. It is a very complex multi–layered plan starting with an infusion of general disbelief in demons followed by a suffocation of distractions to keep us away from God. Satan wants you to believe that he doesn't exist! If you don't believe in an actual devil, then you don't feel the need to put up defenses that shield you from his attacks. It is like leaving the front door wide open in a crime infested neighborhood, with a neon sign on the door that reads, "Come on in and help yourself to everything I own; no resistance will be encountered".

Within the church there are clergy and lay people whom I

have met that have adamantly told me that I am wrong in my "assumption" in believing an actual devil really exists. They even went as far as explaining away my satanic involvement with demons as just self-induced hallucinations. I have photographs documenting marks left on body from physical encounters with a demon that could not have been made by human hands. I have encountered actual demons that made their presence known in very physical ways including being documented on various forms of electronic media. I am a living testimony to how the malice of an actual conjured or summoned up demon is not only far reaching, but also long standing.

If you read the New Testament, you will find scores of scriptures regarding Satan as a real spirit being. The scriptures also offer ways of protecting oneself from the snares of the devil. In I John 3:8 (KJV) we read, "…the devil sinned from the beginning. For this purpose the Son of God was manifested, that he might destroy the works of the devil".

Did our Lord and Savior in the fourth chapter of Matthew lie about his encounter and temptation by Satan in the wilderness? Since Jesus never sinned, there was no way he could have wrestled with the "concept" of the "inherent evil within", because no evil was ever present in Jesus. Jesus spoke and rebuked an actual spirit being during this pivotal temptation. Satan is real! Jesus himself in Matthew 10:28 (KJV) says, "And fear not them which kill the body, but are not able to kill the soul: but rather fear him [the devil] which is able to destroy both soul and body in hell." If Jesus NEVER told us to stop believing in Satan, then who did?

Disbelief in an actual devil allows demons to be an "invisible" negative force in your life wrecking havoc and mayhem without your "seeing" that it is them tormenting you. Trust me, demons squeal with delight when their covert attacks have the person scream out, "Why God are you punishing me?", or "I hate you God for doing this to me". If the evil ones succeed in getting you to not believe in actual demon entities, then the only one left to blame for your misfortunes is God. Not only do demons barge into your life bearing gifts of suffering and discontentment, but they deceive you into blaming God and not demons for their devilish exploits in your life. When it feels like your life is turning in to a Greek tragedy, don't battle God; He isn't the enemy! Recognize and accept who the real enemy is; Satan and his legions of demons.

Satan's Nuclear Arsenal
Lies and Half Truths

By far, this highly effective weapon permeates into every human being today, one way or another. Satan's temperament is defined through lying. John 8:44 describes Satan as a liar and "father of lies". When you are the author of a lie, or knowingly or unknowingly believe and or repeat a lie, you have granted the demons permission to surround and attack you. Untruthfulness of any sort is the "stuff demons feed on". It is a vibrational pattern that mirrors their essence. As they absorb this "energy" of lying emanating from you, they grow stronger as your resolve to commit to the truth grows weaker. Demons will use this "power" to continue the flow of ungodliness from you by convincing you that you will get away with it Scott free. The eigth commandment of "thou shall not lie (bear false witness)", spells out clearly that lying is a sin. Lying is beyond question the most toxic activity we can engage in. Besides it being a complete misrepresentation of the truth, the deep sense of distrust it will leave in its wake can have devastating effects on the person who is on the receiving end of the lie.

Every time we ignore the truth, we ignore God. God is truth. When we lie, God can't be a part of that because He is absolute truth. We don't invite God in by being untruthful; we invite Satan in instead. Lying is a demon's native tongue. When you lie, you are not only speaking the language demons can connect with, but also you are in sync with a demon's nature. Unfortunately, in today's world lying has become second nature to the point we rationalize lying, and consider some forms like white lies, harmless. While lying isn't always a direct attack by a demon, it is one of their most effective ways to separate us from God. In a world that has cocooned itself with deception, it is very difficult to break free and remain truthful for any length of time.

Lying is much more than just a bad habit. The Holy Spirit and Holy Angels including your guardian angel will "step back" a step if you will, when you engage in telling a lie because they refuse to co–habit in your "space" with any hint of evil. You may not think the lie is all that serious or bad, but remember the Holy Angels have witnessed deception at its worst, culminating in the epic heavenly battle of casting out "the father of lies". They have a zero tolerance policy regarding justification of any sin because they are 100% pure truth. Demons will step forward when angels step back. Demons are incapable of being truthful because as I said before, they are 100% evil. Once back in your personal space they will attempt to use rationalization to justify your lie. If they succeed, the initial lie snowballs into more lies, each lie trying to cover the tracks of the previous one. That is why there is no such thing as a "simple lie". Having to keep track of exactly what you said and to whom becomes mentally exhausting, compounded by the guilt of being deceptive, and the fear of being caught in the lie. The individual ends up always "looking over his shoulder" consumed by a spirit of unrest. In this environment of discontentment, the demons grow more powerful as an influence in your life. Jesus himself said in John 8:44(NIV), "He [Satan] was a murderer from the beginning, and does not stand in the truth, because no truth is in him. When he speaks a lie, he speaks from his own resources, for he is a liar and the father of lies."

This is a spiritual battle where there can only be one victor. It is a battle where only you can determine the outcome. Keep on lying and you hand over ground held by the Holy Spirit to the demonic legions who will plunder and pillage their way into your head. Admit to God that you have sinned and ask for His forgiveness and help, and watch as Heaven's Cavalry wielding swords of truth reclaim ground once held by you. As John 8:32 famously states, "The truth shall set you free". This is so less complicated and much more liberating than keeping track of a lie.

What About a "White Lie?"

You are breaking one of the Ten Commandments every time you lie, period! While there are times when a white lie is justified, recognize it for what it still is at the core; a deception. We convince ourselves that under certain conditions telling a lie isn't a sin. If anything, the one you are deceiving is you! Galatians 6:7 (KJV) very strongly states, "Be not deceived; God is not mocked". Demons aren't finicky; they will feed on any deception including white lies. I am guilty of knowingly telling white lies because I don't want the person to suffer undue emotional stress if they can't handle the truth at hand. That doesn't make it right; just justified in my head.

We have exerted so much energy into polishing our white lies that we have not put any effort into researching alternatives to lying. We have become so focused on making a lie believable that we haven't even considered how to present the truth in a constructive manner. Jesus is our model teacher. In a world dominated by evil, Jesus made many enemies by being truthful. In all the gospels not once did he tell a lie of any sort to protect someone's "feelings". He spoke the truth very boldly because Jesus didn't then, and doesn't now, compromise with evil.

I am only presenting you with the facts. Only you can decide how to interpret the validity of telling a lie for the "right" reason. The next time you ponder birthing a lie, first listen to Jesus' warning in Matthew 12:36–37, "But I say to you that for every idle word men speak, they will give account of it in the day of judgment. For by your words you will be justified, and by your words you will be condemned."

A half truth is more dangerous than an outright lie because it leaves out just enough of the truth so as to deceive the person into a false conclusion. To make this practice more palatable, we "sugar coat" it by referring to it as a "half truth" and not a "half lie"; as if that will make it less offensive. A half truth is, at its core, still a lie. Telling a full lie or half truth is the quickest way to nourish a demon. If the lie is an especially "juicy" one, you can bet that the initial demon drawn into your lie will scream out "Buffet!" so as to attract his buddies. Demons are not only pack hunters, but they are also communal feeders.

You can see the impact of demonic feeding in people who are habitual liars. After a while these poor souls can't even distinguish fact from fiction. Anxiety and a sense of desperation cloud their judgment. Habitual liars over time become neurotic from all the energy they expend "looking over their shoulder" hoping a lie doesn't become exposed.

Demons then are in a position to manipulate that person's thoughts because sin (lying) lets them in. When you open your mouth to speak a lie, know that it is Satan and not God doing the talking for you. When you lie you end up as your own prisoner of war. Never forget that ALL forms of deception no matter how well they are presented are nothing more than just lies that are gift wrapped and presented with a bow on top. Satan doesn't put a gun to your head and force you to lie; it is still your choice.

Deception of Faith

Martin Luther once said, "Where God builds a church, the devil builds a chapel next door."

Demons will attempt to distort and pervert scripture to keep you away from the truth! In an age where we have become accustomed to having everything spoon fed to us, using discernment to distinguish godliness from ungodliness seems like too much effort. Demons are counting on your spiritual laziness to deceive the masses. Developing the attitude of just going to Mass once a week so as to meet the minimum requirement for being a Christian, isn't a sin. But by not fostering a daily relationship with God, human nature will listen to the demonic whisperings of self-indulgence and instant gratification. The more distant God becomes to you, the closer the demons slither into your space to infect you with religious apathy.

Whenever a questionable doctrine or practice slips past you unchallenged, you have deserted God's ranks and enlisted in Satan's army! When faced with an error, not reacting at all is just as bad as reacting wrongly. It is complacency at its worst. When you see a fellow parishioner slipping away from the truth, and you don't want to get involved for whatever justification that comes to mind, you are playing into the hands of a demon. In essence by doing nothing you are helping the demons potentially destroy someone else's soul. James 5:19–20 (NIV) offers this advice: "My brothers, if one of you should wander away from the truth and someone should bring him back, remember this: whoever turns a sinner back from the error of his way will save him from death and cover over a multitude of sins."

II Corinthians 11:14–15 states, "And no marvel; for Satan himself is transformed into an angel of light; therefore it is no great thing if his ministers also be transformed as the ministers of righteousness, whose end shall be according to their works." Satan and his minions will use half truths disguised as religion to lure away even those who seek out God.

In chapter two I talked about meeting a born again young man with whom I went to religious revivals and other similar functions. I listened as the preacher in a fevered pitch spoke about the only way to get rid of Satan completely was to be "born again". I did follow his "altar call" at one of these meetings where I "accepted Jesus into my heart as my personal savior". I was considered "born again". This was important to me because I heard the preacher promise that a spirit-filled born again Christian was 100% protected from Satan as long as they walked in obedience to Christ.

Unfortunately, I fell victim to a half truth because I was still being harassed by demons despite my commitment to be a born again Christian. I didn't stay long with this movement because I couldn't handle the arrogance of my fellow believers boast about how they were out of the reach of Satan's attacks. They came across as over confident and cocky in their ability to withstand demonic attacks. I, after having lived through the nightmarish hell of being tormented day and night for months on end, couldn't embrace such a naïve view. It didn't make sense. Jesus, as the Son of God who was without sin, was harassed and attacked by Satan all throughout his ministry. Job was a righteous man who was severely attacked by Satan himself. What exempted the born again believer from demonic attacks? This "doctrine" was a cleverly designed half truth by Satan himself to get these believers to let down their guard in regard to demonic attacks which always resulted in a "blindside" they never saw coming.

The closer to God you are, the more Satan wants to destroy that relationship. The lives of many of our Saints are testimony to this. They were persecuted by men and demons for their faithfulness to God. You were created in the image of God. Since Satan hates God, and your mere presence on earth mirrors an image of Him, you ARE a target and will remain so until the day you die!

St. Joseph as Satan's Real Estate Agent?
One of the most disturbing "practices" occurring among more Catholics than should be, is the practice of burying St. Joseph in order to sell your property. I had only heard of it recently while engaging in a religious conversation with a shop keeper. She, as a non-practicing Catholic, was horrified by this custom and asked my thoughts on it. I searched the internet for information on this observance. I was completely flabbergasted at how wide spread this custom really was. Pages and pages of "how to bury St. Joseph", purchasing a 'kit', and testimonials by the hundreds as to its effectiveness filled my screen. I even found and purchased a booklet in a Catholic book store promoting this form of sacrilege. The shop keeper even felt I was "over-reacting" when I became

indignant over this practice. More than two million St. Joseph real estate kits are sold each year in the United States. This "superstition" dates back to the medieval times to a practice called "degradation of the saints". In essence back then, images or statues were insulted until their tormentor's request was granted.

What really made me gasp is the growing trend to bury a statue of St. Joseph upside down (as opposed to the earlier custom of right side up) on your property so that it will sell. Once you bury him, you recite a prayer which reads more like a ransom note. There were lots of variations on the prayer to be recited, but this one was the most popular: "Oh St. Joseph, guardian of household needs, we know you don't like to be upside down in the ground, but the sooner our escrow closes, the sooner we will dig you up and put you in a place of honor in our new home."

While many fellow Catholics and even some clergy may feel this is a harmless way of petitioning a Saint, I will not stay silent on what reeks of a satanic ritual! Holy objects such as statues, rosaries, and depictions of any heavenly images are a sacred representation of the God family. These "images" help us "visualize" an image of God in our limited brains and should be treated with respect. I Timothy 4:7 (KJV) clearly states such practices are wrong: "But **refuse** profane and old wives fables, and exercise thyself rather unto godliness."

Statues of Saints remind us of the lives of ordinary people who didn't stay silent when it came to doing God's will, and serve as roles model for us today. Many sacrificed their lives for God, and deserve to be remembered with honor. When we petition the Saints to help intercede on our behalf, it should be done with humility and reverence, on our knees in a spirit of gratitude. How dare anyone "threaten" and torment a Saint in such a manner and for material gain no less!! It is nothing other than sacrilegious. I know it is an established "practice" among many Catholics, but that doesn't make it right. You can't serve two masters at the same time. Jesus always talked about storing our treasures up in heaven and not in some bank account here on earth. Colossians 2:8 (KJV) warns, "Beware lest any man spoil you through philosophy and vain deceit, **after the traditions of men, after the rudiments of the world**, and not after Christ."

In the Satanic Black Mass, holy objects including statues and the crucifix over the altar are always inverted (turned upside down). This is done to desecrate all holiness. It is done to mock God and all holy beings. When I tried to find out when and how the inversion burial of St. Joseph began, I could not find any shred of evidence at all. It appears to have started out of thin air. Since Satan is the god of this world, he basically controls our financial institutions and commerce. Burying St. Joseph upside down is regarded as much more effective than right side up, as testimonials of quick sales litter the internet like strewn garbage along the freeway median strips. Think about it: Satan offers financial bribes in the form of real estate sales to people willing to desecrate sacred representations of Saints, and all too quickly he is finding eager and willing converts. It is a mass seduction as now Protestants and even pagans are engaging in this practice.

Like Judas who sold out Jesus for thirty pieces of silver, many people today are selling out God (by this practice) for successfully closed escrow accounts. You can literally sugar coat a deadly poison so it looks like candy, but it will kill you as quickly as if it were in its raw form. Make no mistake about it; people who engage in this practice are carrying out, albeit unknowingly, a satanic ritual right out of the Black Mass. By following this practice, people are accidently opening up their homes to demonic influences because demons are attracted by familiar rituals. Instead, people should have a blessed statue of St. Joseph placed in their home, light a candle in front of him, and pray in full humility to St. Joseph to intercede on their behalf to Almighty God to help them with this petition, IF IT IS GOD'S WILL. Then follow the old adage of, "Let go and Let God". Take to heart the admonition in I Thessalonians 5:22, "Abstain from all appearances of evil."

Suicide and Depression:
Demonic Coercion

Suicide is increasing in this country at an alarming rate especially among the teenage population. It is another weapon of mass destruction employed by the evil ones to separate us from the love of God. Suicide is an act that Satan knows causes God great sorrow. Feeling so hopeless that you abandon all attempts to reach out to heaven is a frontal assault by a powerful demon. Feeling like a failure and becoming overwhelmed by life's challenges is a devilish strategy designed to consume you with despair and a sense of no way out. The demon is under direct orders from Satan to get you to stop believing in God's healing love by trapping you with depression, guilt, and isolation. Depression's main power hold over you is to sway you into believing that you have no value to anyone including God, so therefore God has abandoned you. Guilt refuses forgiveness. Like an infected wound that festers, guilt allows Satan's message to seep and pool deep within our soul unobstructed by hope.

Depression evicts love from our soul. It is a feeling of total loss and worthlessness. This demonic assault if not combated could lead those souls down the path to suicide. In the moment of your deepest despair you can rest assured that the demons are rejoicing!! After all, their entire goal is to cut you off from God any way they can and by any means. If you do this willingly, you can bet they are doing a goose stepping victory dance in your honor. Unreal expectations that dominate our outlook on life aren't imaginary; they are demonic whisperings into your subconscious setting you up purposely to feel like a failure! A demon tries to coax you into an obsessive personality because that creates tunnel vision. Your focus becomes so narrow that you lose all objectivity. Lose objectivity and it will shut out God because you won't be able to see the big picture of God's overall plan for your life.

There are two types of debilitating depression: chemical imbalance and demonic. The first type of depression requires a thorough evaluation by a health care professional to ensure that there aren't any underlying medical causes such as a chemical imbalance in the brain which can be treated with medications. The second type of depression is demonically induced brought on by that individual opening himself up to an upper level demon or gang of lesser demons. This type of depression manifests on the outside the same way clinical depression would, but its root cause isn't medically treatable. A lower level demon by itself does not have the magnitude of persuasion required for such an assault, but if a bunch of them band together and attack the person en masse, that poor soul is in dire straits. I will discuss this in more detail in a later chapter. Demonic assaults of this severity require intensive spiritual counseling to guide the individual back to God. This sort of demonically induced depression is designed to exterminate any capacity for receiving or giving unconditional love. Unconditional love is the essence of God. When we practice unconditional love, we are imitating God's nature. It is what sends a demon fleeing away from us writhing in pain, because any godly trait is a torment to them.

Suicide is a terrible tragedy that devastates those left behind. The agony of, "If only I…" that torments a family member or friend predisposes them to mental demonic hostage taking. Beating yourself up for not acting sooner, or doing more, is in fact subconsciously convincing yourself that you are a failure. I too lost a close friend to suicide. The feelings of not being able to stop the tragedy unfairly took a toll on my self-esteem. Remember in the end NO ONE is responsible for someone else's suicide. That responsibility and choice belongs solely to the one contemplating death. DON'T LET A DEMON CONVINCE YOU OTHERWISE!!!

The demons will linger around the survivors hoping to capitalize on the guilt and anger generated by such an untimely death. The overwhelming sense of loss and unfairness opens the doorway for demons to our thoughts. They will then attempt to attack the survivors by flooding them with thoughts of guilt. Just like the finale of a fireworks display, demons will implant so many guilt thoughts at once, that it is hard to recognize who the authors of such guilt feelings are. Being bombarded like that with an overkill of guilt clouds objectivity and gives demons access to plant thoughts of anger against God and not Satan who is the evil mastermind behind suicide.

All life is a gift from God and to take one's life prematurely is stealing that gift away from Him. Jesus offered His life as the perfect sacrifice and atonement for ALL our sins. By His sacrifice we are freed from the bondage of sin and the devil. It was your cross that Jesus shouldered as He made the agonizing trek to Calvary. He died for your sins so that you wouldn't have to. Killing yourself because you are haunted by the sins you have committed, feeling unworthy of love, or feeling there is no place for you in this world is both unnecessary and needless. The ultimate victory for a demon is to watch us self-destruct because of his lies and not God's truths. Suicide requires free will because no matter how hopeless a situation may seem, it is still a voluntary choice. God offers us life while Satan offers us death. Suicide means accepting Satan's lies as absolute truth. Death by suicide is a demon's ultimate trophy. Every time a lost soul dies by their own hand, the demon stands over that corpse, looks up to God and flips Him the middle finger in defiance. If this last statement sounds vulgar and offensive, then I have given you the most accurate visual possible.

I want to reach out to anyone who is contemplating suicide for any reason and let them know they aren't alone. God is here to help you and He does that by working through people. Reach out and know someone will reach back to you. Don't allow a demon to do a victory dance over your corpse. You may feel like you are totally powerless over anything in your life and I am here to tell you that's a demonic lie. By depriving a demon from rejoicing over your death, you are receiving power from all the angels surrounding you, sent there by the Blessed Mother and God to give you the strength to fight through their convincing lies. When you realize that suicide isn't the only option, and it is a demonic attack, then your life has already begun to turn around for the good. Know that unhealthy emotions don't have to corner us into feeling there is no way out. Unhealthy emotions let us know that we are on a self-destructive path. They serve to remind us to get back on track. See the value in these emotions as a tool to re–examine your perceptions, and don't embrace the destructive power they are capable of.

Distractions:
The "A–Bomb" of Demonic Weapons

Demons will resort to any means to keep you from having an active relationship with God. One of their most powerful weapons they deploy against us is that of distractions. Busy lives, television, career advancement, and social media all are easily manipulated by demons to keep us too busy to maintain a close relationship with God. If you are too busy to go to church for one hour a week because there aren't enough hours in the day to get everything done, well then your priorities are managed by Satan. If you are too tired, too busy, or too depressed to worship and praise the Creator of the universe, you are under a definite demonic attack designed to hinder you from nurturing a relationship with God.

The evil ones are influencing our culture through media advertising with commercials promoting self-indulgence as a reward for a hectic paced life. I even remember a television commercial that used the expression of "sinfully delicious" to describe some dessert. The advertising industry is all about money. Product honesty is diminished when profit margins are king. This mindset is a breeding ground for attracting and sustaining legions of demons. Demons influence commercials to broadcast their message of self-indulgence subliminally. It is brainwashing our culture to obsess on our every want and desire. Add to that the fact that television and movies are a demon's pulpit to promote casual sex, and violent crime as the accepted societal norm. How many "feel good", morally sound family movies score an Oscar award these days?

Entitlement Should be the Eighth Deadly Sin

The demons have patiently and slowly infused into our society over the last few decades a spirit that the total pursuit of self-happiness is the goal of life. The problem with this half truth is the fact; total happiness is based not on a spiritual communion with God and respect for our fellow man, but solely on material gain, instant gratification, and saturation of physical pleasures which excludes God. Being godly or religious is becoming increasingly viewed by our society as a hindrance to obtaining and experiencing our every heart's desire because morality would get in the way. This demonically wicked principle of destroying Christian ethics incorporates the seven deadly sins as the basis for this mass corruption: lust, gluttony, greed, sloth, wrath, envy, and pride. The focus of the fallen angels is to convince you to believe that you are a god in human form and as a result deserve to have the world bow down before your feet. You are the master and creator of your own destiny and not God is their subliminal message to you.

This demonic tactic has bred into our subconscious a sense of entitlement. Animal behaviorists have even come close to this truth with their new and extremely controversial theory called the, "Hundredth Monkey Effect". I looked it up in Wikipedia on the internet and basically this effect states that a learned behavior, once enough monkeys engage in it, will spread instantaneously from one related monkey group to another. It basically alludes to some sort of supernatural instantaneous spreading of a learned behavior if enough monkeys do it even if there is no direct monkey to monkey communication. In human terms we can apply this same principle to the term "societal norm". Somewhere, and somehow, almost "magically", look how our societal values have diminished over the last fifty to sixty years.

Abortion, gay marriage, and sex on television were taboo in the 1950's. Can we pinpoint an exact date when this all changed? No. How did it all change to the point that these ungodly principles are now accepted as common behavior in our country? The "supernatural" aspect of this spreading is nothing more than the higher, former choir of fallen angels' globally spreading ungodliness en masse through the subliminal message of, "If it feels good, do it!"

This philosophy allows for moral laxity in the pursuit of self-centered physical happiness. It is so subtle we don't see this evil strategy unfold on a daily basis.

I would also like to point out that this same "effect" can be a positive one too. Never forget that despite the fact this earth is swarming with demons looking to destroy us in every way possible, heavenly angels are sent by God to watch over us too. If enough of us were to take the Blessed Mother's continued admonitions of praying and turning back to her son to heart, angels, and not demons would dominate our air waves. In Jeremiah 4:1–2, God offers a promise to us collectively as a nation if we embrace spiritual values instead of selfish ones; "O Israel, come back to me", says the Lord. "If you throw away your detestable idols and go astray no more, and if you will swear by my name alone, and begin to live good, honest lives and uphold justice, then you will be a blessing to the nations of the world, and all the people will come and praise my name." As Christians we are spiritual Israelites, and our country proclaims itself to still be Christian in nature, so this promise is still valid today as it was back in Jeremiah's time. Remember the law of free will dictates that we have to choose to accept good or evil. Choose godliness and heaven will be your strongest ally; choose ungodliness and demons will be your worst enemy.

You don't have to look far to see evidence of this satanic indoctrination of entitlement; it has infected our society, including our youth. How many children today would voluntarily give up their cell phone, iPad, laptop, and the latest in fashion? How many people do you know that "live for the weekend" so that they can party all weekend long or turn driving around for yard sales into a compulsive obsession? How many people take for granted medical insurance at their job, expecting it, rather than being grateful that their company offers it? How much do you take for granted in a day's time? In II Timothy 3:1–6 we see how in the last days many will embrace the seven deadly sins: "But mark this: There will be terrible times in the last days. People will be lovers of themselves, lovers of money, boastful, proud, abusive, disobedient to their parents, ungrateful, unholy, without love, unforgiving, slanderous, without self -control, brutal, not lovers of the good, treacherous, rash, conceited lovers of pleasure rather than God—having a form of godliness but denying its power. Have nothing to do with them."

Harboring a sense of entitlement incorporates all the seven deadly sins. The individual feels that they "deserve" everything they desire, and they feel entitled to all the pleasures life has to offer for the satisfaction of their physical needs. Everyone has their own demons to battle, so don't make it easier for demons to pollute your mind by becoming totally deceived into believing you have a "right" to something. This perverted ethic is so in harmony with a demon's mindset that it becomes difficult over time to distinguish between a demonically planted thought and the individual's own thought. Scientists believe that the average human being thinks up better than 60,000 thoughts per day. That is 60,000 chances every day for the rest of your life for a demon to plant a thought to see if it will take root.

Demons are very clever; they know the possibility of a euphoric high that results in overindulgence so they will be relentless in enticing us to "indulge" in our deepest hidden physical desire. Paul in Galatians 5:19–21 warned us about the dangers of the seven deadly sins; "The acts of the sinful nature are obvious: sexual immorality, impurity and debauchery, idolatry and witchcraft; hatred, discord jealousy, fits of rage, selfish ambition, dissentions, factions and envy, drunkenness, orgies, and the like. I warn you, as I did before, that those who live like this will not inherit the kingdom of God."

Keep in mind "splurging" conotates moderation which is ok, and isn't the same thing as indulging which uses no self-control. Remember, demons are never far away from you and are always waiting for an opening YOU provide them to gain a foothold in your head. Engaging in the seven heavenly virtues of: chastity, temperance, charity, diligence, patience, kindness, and humility, will create a hostile work environment for any demon that has weaseled his way into your head. Humility in all you speak and do is an especially powerful weapon against pride which is a powerful vice created by Lucifer himself!

If you want to personally kick some demon booty, I have a fast acting tactic that will work instantly. Entitlement is our society's opium. It is what demons spoon feed us to keep us addicted to the pursuit of worldly pleasures. Feeling that you have a "right" to something, in essence means you are demanding that whatever that "something" is, it be handed over to you NOW. Break that habit! Practice the virtue of gratitude. Be grateful for what you already have without the expectation of more. It will help you see that life is a gift from God and not an expectation. Heed the words in Colossians 2:6–7 (NIV), "So then, just as you received Christ

Jesus as Lord, continue to live in him, rooted and built up in him, strengthened in the faith as you were taught, and overflowing with thankfulness (gratitude)." By adopting an attitude of gratitude, I guarantee that your outlook on the meaning of life, and your purpose on earth will change for the better. This will have the demons retreating in disgust from your space. Practicing this virtue of gratitude is the first step of empowerment; taking back control of your life from demons means you are no longer a slave to the demonic spirit of entitlement. "Be imitators of God, therefore, as dearly loved children and live a life of love, just as Christ loved us and gave himself up for us as a fragrant offering and sacrifice to God." (Ephesians 5:1–2, NIV)

Once you begin to embrace gratitude, you will see the world in a more positive light. Instead of focusing on what you don't have in life, look for God in everyone you meet. The more you find evidence of it no matter how insignificant or small, you will draw closer to God. When I see a stranger entering the post office and waiting to hold open the door for me as I enter, I know I have found evidence of God. Random acts of kindness aren't isolated occurrences, but affirmations from heaven that God is with you! Try performing random acts of kindness. By doing so, you are a personal witness to the world and demons of the FACT that God is alive and manifesting Himself daily in our lives. Jesus himself admonished us to practice kindness in Matthew 5:6, "let your light shine before men, that they may see your good deeds and praise your Father in heaven".

Addictions:
Demonic Hostage Taking
The definition of self-indulgence is basically defined as indulgence of one's own desires without restraint. When

cravings turn into compulsions, self-control is temporarily suspended. Our brain is continually thinking thoughts for most of our waking hours and even when we sleep (thoughts are brought up to the surface through dreams). Thoughts aren't the product of some physical bodily function, we create them. We aren't mindless mentally numb zombie like drones who wander around on auto pilot. There is always someone in control at the helm of our cognitive "ship" directing the course of thoughts. When a person becomes addicted, it is demons who take control of the helm of the ship.

Addictions are demonic infestations. The perverted or insatiable lusting and compulsion for a particular substance or action are the cravings of the demons and not you! What you are acting out are the demon's desires and not your own. Why else would a person feel remorse, shame, and guilt after such indulgence? The trademark of addiction is that the individual lies so much to hide his addiction that he can't be trusted. Relationships break and fall apart. Such miserable feelings are all the byproducts of evil.

Let me be clear: addictions are NOT automatic infestations by demons. Demons can't force a person to engage in anything without the individual consenting to it first. If, while tempted, the person gives in to the temptation, then and only then can the demons begin to manipulate the person's mind. The reality is that the only one that can cause you to sin is YOU!! Demons can only seduce you, but you have free will to resist or not resist.

The truth is, ALL evil inevitably always self-destructs. Use this truth as discernment when faced with engaging in a behavior or activity. What is the end result? If I go to this frat party, will I engage in philosophic conversations with others about global warming, or, will everyone get so drunk that they end up passed out on the floor? If I engage in this argument with my spouse, will it bring about a peaceful conclusion or personal regret over carelessly chosen spiteful words? If you are saying to yourself right now, "Well I don't have a problem with my drinking, gambling, shopping, working, etc.", ask yourself what the end result would be of your engaging in that act. If there are feelings of regret, guilt, and a wake of discontentment and arguments with family and friends, then see that you are under attack by not one, but many demons.

Demons are so skilled in manipulating and using our disappointments and hurts against us, that they convince us that we and not them are responsible for this self-induced misery.

The hallmark of demonically induced addiction is that the person feels powerless and compelled to engage in a certain behavior, despite the cost emotionally, physically, and spiritually. As the addiction takes over controlling every aspect of a person's life, demons plant the thought of self -hatred. Self-hatred is a very effective demonic tool because it creates an unending cycle of destructive thoughts and actions. Self-hatred over not wanting to do it, but doing it anyway. Self-hatred over feeling like a failure in life. Self-hatred over losing touch with God. Self-hatred becomes the motivation for the self-destructive behavior.

The reality of addiction is that the demons have convinced you of a lie. The individual isn't addicted to a particular substance or behavior, but they are addicted to pain. The pain of traumatic events, the pain of low self-esteem, the pain of being victimized by abuse, are all forms of emotional agony. The substance or behavior is just the method used (unknowingly or knowingly) to express this powerful feeling and escape reality even if it is only temporary. Addictive personalities aren't constitutionally weak individuals who over indulge in a variety of things. The infestation of demons in that person's life convinces them that they are so unworthy of love and so therefore they deserve only pain. When such a cluster of demons take hold in a person's mind they will flood them with negative thoughts which generate negative emotions which predisposes them to giving into their cravings. This leads to feelings of shame and remorse over not being able to break the vicious cycle.

Demonic hostage taking is fortified with fail safes to prevent the person from seeing that letting go of unresolved painful or traumatic issues, distant or current, is the way to recovery. The first and powerful demonic fail-safe is denying the addiction. "I can handle it" statements are manifestations of demonic thought manipulation. The demons convince you that those who notice and bring to your attention this destructive behavior are "out to get you", or don't understand you. Anyone who confronts an individual about their addiction is perceived as a threat. Addicts will begin to isolate themselves from people and that is exactly what the demons want! They don't want outside interference ruining their plan of total self-destruction of the individual they are tormenting.

The second demonic fail-safe is the "I can always quit tomorrow" statement. The problem though, is that tomorrow never comes. It is a cruel irony employed by the demons to plant thoughts that tomorrow will be a new beginning, and then make sure that temptations are so overwhelming that the person succumbs to them. Remember the person in the throes of addiction is reacting to demonic influences from demons that have set up shop in their head. If you don't believe me, try telling an active addict about the love of God and watch them react extremely negatively. You are not hearing the person voicing his/her anger and or hatred against God; it is the demon's thoughts that the addict is manifesting.

Generally people of their own accord don't "hate" God. They may be angry at Him, or deny His existence all together, but actually "hating" God isn't a human emotion. Only Satan and his minions truly hate God. People who vehemently emphasize that they hate God are definitely directly expressing the feelings of a demon. Whenever I come across someone spouting out how much they hate God, and I can't get them to see that their reasoning is flawed, I know I am dealing with a person who is mentally connected with a demon. In my experience the individuals I have met who truly expressed hatred towards God were people trapped in an addiction. I don't look upon them in disgust. I have great compassion for them instead. I understand the source of their mental torment that consumes them day in and day out. Pray for them and never stop reaching out to someone battling addiction. They might refuse your help a hundred times, but only one time is needed to start the road to recovery. Only one time where a word or sentence you speak acts as a catalyst and gets the person to realize they don't have to live under that demonic bondage anymore. Twelve step recovery groups are God's way of intervening in an addict's life. They truly are "heaven sent".

The good news is that God so loves every one of us, he won't allow us to self-destruct without first trying to get through to us an infinite number of times. Your free will determines whether to block God's attempt to reach out to you. Free will can only block God's attempt. God will never stop trying despite our obstinacy. God didn't create us as a lab rat to test just how strong our willpower is, or find our breaking point. He created us as His children. We are here on earth not to endure a life of misery, but learn lessons that teach us the appreciation of eternal life. Many times God intervenes directly in our lives through others. Interventions set up by concerned friends and family are orchestrated by God. It is God reaching out His hand to rescue you from whatever anguish the demons have falsely convinced you is unchangeable. Be open to God and His opportunities to work life altering miracles in your life. As a Christian you MUST believe God when demons try to convince you that your life is a train wreck. Take a personal interest in EVERY choice you make. By doing this you are taking back the mental and spiritual control held for way too long by the demons.

"Everything is permissible but not everything is beneficial. Everything is permissible but not everything is constructive. Nobody should seek their own good, but the good of others." I Corinthians 10:23–24.

Chapter 8

Just How Did I Manage to Attract a Cluster of Demons Anyway?

By far the easiest way to attract a demon or a cluster of demons is through the act of sinning. Every time you sin it is a personal invitation to a demon to enter your space. Demons study our behavior and monitor impure expressed desires; keeping track of us through the trail of the effects of sin we leave behind us. While we can be released from the eternal effects of sin through repentance, we are bound by the consequences of sin in our physical lives.

We can't undo the ramifications of a sin we commit against someone else. You can't resurrect a murdered victim, or rebuild a marriage destroyed by infidelity. Sin destroys more than just the person who commits the sin. It leaves scars on relationships, careers, self-worth, and obliterates trust. It is like ringing a dinner bell for demons to join in on the feast of ungodliness. The more you sin, the more control you hand over to demons. Demons thrive in, and are fortified by unconfessed sins. They flock in droves to an individual who is living in a perpetual state of sin. When you commit a sin you present demons with a golden opportunity they cannot and will not pass up; to be able to inflict pain in your life. Demons as spirit beings aren't bogged down with hectic careers and families. They don't eat nor sleep nor grow tired and weary. Unlike our human bodies, as spirits they never age. What this means for you is that demons have unlimited energy and all the time in the world to devote in making you their object of desire.

When is a Sin Really a Sin?

Don't be blindsided by the tactic demons use through religious legalism to lead you into believing that sin can be divided into big or little sins, with the "little" sins not personally needing to be individually identified, examined, and confessed. There is no sliding scale of spiritual danger when it comes to the "types" of sins we are committing. All sin (big and little) is equally deadly to your spiritual life. The problem with this demonic "philosophy" of minimizing venial sins is that over time denial replaces guilt in our conscience. This confuses us into believing the venial sin is justified and no longer sinful. We then deny the reality of "trivial" sins as being harmful to our spirituality.

Adopting this mindset not only hardens our conscience, but provides a rich and nurturing environment for multiple demonic entities to infiltrate your thoughts, reasoning capacity, and worship of God. The knowledge that a million venial (minor) sins won't keep you out of heaven (but they will put you in purgatory) isn't an excuse to continue committing the same sin over and over again. The demons will try to whisper, "Go ahead and commit that same little sin again.

You can always confess it away later at Mass. This sin isn't enough to keep you out of heaven, so indulge and offer a quick apology to God when the mood strikes you. Why aim for perfection at all, seeing there is a high probability that you will end up in purgatory anyway." When you begin to feel that venial sins aren't deadly to your spiritual life, well then I will be the first to tell you that you are under the influence of a demon. This attitude draws in multiple demonic entities all wanting a chance to pervert your spiritual walk with God. Jesus himself warned us about the danger of sin when he said in John 8:34, "I tell you the truth, everyone who sins is a slave to sin".

My spiritual director gave me the perfect analogy of just how venial sins can lead to our spiritual destruction. Compare a venial sin to a fly on the screen of your porch window. The fly is only a speck on the screen which isn't obstructing your view at all. It is easily remedied by swatting the fly with a fly swatter. A venial sin is in the same way like a fly on the screen (in terms of it not clouding our spiritual vision) and can be easily remedied in a similar fashion. With a spiritual "fly swatter" either confess this sin to a priest or offer up a sincere apology to God with the intention of not trying to commit it again. Now let's say there is a swarm of flies on the screen window. The sheer mass of all these "little" flies is too much to handle with a fly swatter. The view out of the window is almost completely obstructed. Hitting this gigantic mass with a fly swatter will only cause the flies to disperse all over the room creating an even bigger problem of eradicating them. If you "collect" enough little sins, your spiritual vision will in the same manner also be obstructed and the "sin" will disperse into other areas of your life. It won't be as easy to break free from that sin because it has become habitual and you don't "see" it as harmful. Demons know we are creatures of habit and will try to hook you with a little sin because they know your weaknesses. They want to create a state of habitual sin within you. They know a venial sin won't keep you out of heaven, but enough of them combined will negatively impact how you relate to God. Habitual unremorseful sinning attracts clusters of demons to you.

Take for example the sin of stealing. You are probably thinking right now, "Well this doesn't apply to me because I have never stolen a car, money, or objects from anyone, nor would I."

Have you ever called in "sick" to work for reasons other than actually being sick? Besides committing the sin of lying you are in fact "stealing" time away from your boss. You agreed to a five day work week in the terms of employment. As a gesture of goodwill, your boss provides you with "x" amount of paid sick days so that you can stay home and care for your illness or injury should they occur. At the end of the fiscal year any unused sick days will be lost so you think, "I need to use up my sick days before I lose them, so I will take a sick day here and one there." That is a form of stealing! You are taking time away from the amount of time you agreed to give your employer.

Or how many of you have taken home office supplies such as a pen or note paper without asking permission first? It might seem trivial, but that too is a form of stealing and breaking of one of the commandments. What I am trying to point out here is the fact that not seeing this type of activity as sinful gives demons a stronghold to enter and begin to manipulate your reasoning capabilities. Remember a few chapters back when I talked about the law of attraction where like attracts like? Well the law of attraction equals the law of invitation, or simply put, "you let them in when you sin".

In my ministry working with individuals plagued by a demonic haunting I always ask just how frequently the individual goes to confession. All too often I hear justification over not needing to go for venial (minor) sins. While Catholic doctrine doesn't make it obligatory to go to a priest for the confession of venial (as opposed to a mortal sin) sins because we confess them during the Penitential Rite at Mass, there is also no church doctrine that says we shouldn't seek out the act of confession with a priest for only venial sins. The "I confess…" we recite during Mass provides forgiveness from the non-mortal sins we already committed; not for the ones we have yet to commit. You can leave church as pure as the driven snow but that state doesn't last very long because of our sinful nature.

After you commit a sin there is no waiting period required for demons to accept this invitation you put out there to begin tormenting you. The first sin has the domino effect where the initial sin gives way to more sin. Paul eloquently states how difficult it is to stay unstained by sin for any length of time in Romans 7:18–20 (NIV), "I know that nothing good lives in me, that is, in my sinful nature. For I have the desire to do what is good, but I cannot carry it out. For what I do is not the good I want to do; no, the evil I do not want to do– this I keep on doing. Now if I do what I do not want to do, it is no longer I who do it, but it is sin living in me that does it."

A demon attracted by the "scent" of you having committed a sin will seize the opportunity to take the circumstances that produced the sin and reproduce those circumstances so to seduce you into committing the same sin again and again. This is a tactic that he will exploit until you become a slave to that peculiar sin and now can't break the pattern. Once "hooked" and in bondage to that particular sin, the perpetual state of sin (habitual sinner) now attracts other demons as well. As they gather around such an individual, each demon will impart its own preference for perversion of godliness. These poor souls end up committing sins in other areas of their lives due to the cluster of demons now in control of their reasoning facilities.

When you become addicted to a specific sin you will feel a sense of instant gratification and pleasure. This "feeling" allows the demons permission to entice you into mortal sins. Let me say this very clearly: you don't need to draw up and sign a formal pact with the devil to get his attention; you have already signed on the dotted line with repeated unconfessed and unrepented sins. Demons feel entitled to destroy your soul with whatever evil means they can conceive of. Paul in Romans 6:1–2 strongly advised against the justification of sin, "What shall we say then? Shall we go on sinning so that grace may increase? By no means! We died to sin; how can we live it any longer?"

Justification:
The Most Successful Demonic Strategy for Sin
Beware of one of the most successful demonic traps on the justification of sin. It is better known to you and me as "excuses". By far the most common excuse for sin is thinking we can get away with it because there are no witnesses to our action. I hate to be the realist here, but when you think no one is watching, you have the entire spiritual world looking on as you commit that sin. It may be done in secret when you are alone well hidden from human eyes but I assure you both heavenly eyes and demonic eyes have seen every second of what you have done. Demons convince you that you got away with it because immediately after committing that sin you weren't struck down by a lightning bolt from heaven, there were no human witnesses, and you weren't

pelted with fire and brimstone as a punishment.

Another increasingly popular "excuse" is playing the "genetics" card. Here people will justify their pattern of sin by blaming family genetics as the result of their sin. "Because it is genetic, it is therefore impossible for me to change the behavior... I was born that way" the individual will claim. Scientists may have proved genetically that alcoholism and homosexuality have a genetic link because they have identified genes associated with alcohol excess and sexual orientation, but identifying a gene doesn't justify indulgence in that genetic "variable".

I come from a long family history of alcoholism on my father's side. I grew up in an alcoholic home. I may or may not have genetic markers that point to the high probability that I am prone to alcoholism, but I do have free will to choose to engage or not engage in such behavior. I might be predisposed to alcoholism but self-taught healthy spiritual coping mechanisms for stress is enough to sustain me now where I don't need to drink myself into a stupor. In my past where alcohol got the best of me, I couldn't blame my drinking on anyone but myself. I used it as a coping mechanism because my self-esteem was so low that I felt I had no spiritual value to anyone including God so why bother fighting an easy "fix" to a problem. I was then mentally, spiritually, and emotionally too lazy to fight my addiction.

We create our own pain when we choose to commit sin. Addictions are controlled by a cluster of demons that specialize in that type of perverted mind set. Just like the person predisposed to diabetes who engages in a healthy lifestyle to avert the onset of the disease, we too, no matter what genetic markers say, can circumvent sinful behaviors linked to our genes.

There is a scripture passage in the bible that basically says that the sins of the father are visited upon his children. That shouldn't be interpreted in the sense that whatever wrong doings the father commits, the kids will be punished for it. What that scripture refers to is a belief system. If the father for instance beats up his wife in front of his children, and the mother makes excuses for her husband to her children, then these little ones begin to see this as "normal" interpersonal relationships. It is a great responsibility to be a role model for a child because children will imitate the behaviors, actions, and habits of those who care for them. Growing up in an alcoholic family where excessive daily drinking was typical, I came to the belief that drinking to excess was "normal". When my life began to spiral out of control due to my alcohol excess, it wasn't because I was paying for my father's sins, but because I was engaging in the same behaviors I had observed in him while I grew up. I adopted his belief that alcoholism was something you openly joked about and never took serious.

Demons constantly bait us with opportunities to sin just like a hunter who sets out bait for deer while he sits in a tree waiting to shoot the unsuspecting deer. Demons as pack hunters will gather by the "baiting station" and wait in eager anticipation to see if we are seduced by their "bait" to sin. Sin cuts us off from God and after a while of giving into our sinful nature, we do feel the ramifications of this separation from God. It manifests itself as a general discontent with life where we feel there is something missing from our existence but we can't pinpoint what that is. It may be just that the cluster of venial sins you are denying, are attracting the cluster of demons to you giving you that general discontented feeling. That feeling of discontentment could be your guardian angel whispering to you that you need a course correction leading back to God.

No matter how "trivial" a sin may seem to you, once you recognize that it is a sin, immediately confess it with a spirit of humility and remorse to God or a priest. That alone is a very effective weapon that will keep demonic clusters from gaining a foothold. Just don't expect that a certain behavior or sin will be gone immediately. That is a set up by demons to convince you that it is impossible to break free from that particular sin or behavior. It will take time to overcome ingrained thoughts and behaviors. Breaking free of a habitual sin will take courage and fortitude. Be aware and brace yourself against withdrawal pains from a particular ingrained sinful habit. You can't break the influence of this demonic cluster by yourself. Ask God, Jesus, Our Lady, the Saints, and your guardian angels for help. And remember too; once confessed, sins should serve as teachers and not tormentors! Become consciously aware of taking back control by saying out loud: "From now on things will be different. I am going to break this unbreakable sinful habit with God's help." By saying it out loud you send a clear message back to the demons that you are taking back control. It also serves as an audible affirmation to you (like a pep talk) of your commitment to eradicate that particular ingrained sin. I also cannot stress enough the importance of going to confession with a priest regularly: at least once a month. Admitting out loud your sin to another human being makes it much harder to internalize it as "not so bad".

Demonic Clusters are Tantalized by the Scent of Anger

Anger is an emotion by choice that demons will manipulate. It can be a sudden outburst of strong negative emotion in reaction to a perceived wrong or injustice committed against us. We express anger as a means to correct the situation that is offending us, yet the expression of anger itself does the exact opposite. It is an emotional reaction based on the fear that we are losing control of a situation. When anger is directed at someone and they respond back in kind, it only serves to reinforce the belief that we stand to lose "something".

Anger draws in demons like blood does for sharks. Because it is a very powerful emotion that emits negative energy, it resonates with demons. Demons thrive and do their best work in an atmosphere charged with anger. The first tactic they will employ to escalate this negative energy is to prevent you from exploring the logical and rational side of things. They do this by planting thoughts that evoke powerful emotional responses within you thereby clouding your judgment. Take for example an argument between a wife and husband. The husband comes home late from work and the wife who becomes angry over his late arrival snaps, "Where have you been?" The husband may pause for a couple of seconds so as to formulate a response. Believe it or not demons work fast. In that pause of only a few seconds, demonically planted thoughts go through the wife's head such as, "His pause means he is hiding something. He's out gallivanting while I slave at home. I bet he is having an affair. What lame excuse is he going to try to come up with?" As the husband begins to explain, the wife has convinced herself that the suspicion of an affair (without any supporting facts) is indeed valid and refuses to listen to reason and rejects all of his explanatory statements as lies.

As the wife was waiting for her husband's arrival, she began to have negative thoughts. This attracted a demon who quickly planted a thought of an affair. This thought took hold and now in her head she was envisioning his coming in the door looking guilty. In her head she plays out how the explanation of his tardiness will unfold. The more she dwells on it, the angrier she becomes as she begins to assume how her husband will reply. Demons bank on us reacting out of sheer emotion. Before the husband even got home, she had charged, tried, and found him guilty of an affair based solely on her obsessing over how he responded in the argument she visualized in her mind.

To assume essentially means we are guessing. Without knowing all the facts we end up making up the missing pieces based solely on our perception of the situation. Demanding an explanation without having all the facts offers a demon the chance to insert irrational and/or suspicious negative thoughts into your mind. The person on the receiving end of all this will naturally become defensive and may verbally retaliate with inflammatory remarks. Now that person draws in a demon and we have two demons manipulating both individual's thoughts. In the heat of an argument neither party is in control of the situation. We become controlled like puppets by demonic puppeteers who manipulate the strings causing us to move and react in ways we normally wouldn't.

Arguments in public places with observing onlookers attract clusters of demons that sense the negative emotions of fear, anger, apprehension and confusion of the bystanders. Demons will surround us with people who will distract us from utilizing holy principles for daily living. In particular, demonic clusters get a lot of mileage out of arguments and fights between players at sporting events. Ever notice how the crowds begin to cheer on the fight? Hoards of demons converging on the argument, attracted by the collective negative energy of the spectators infiltrate the thoughts of those habitual sinners and those with unconfessed sins. Sin allows a demon the deepest access to our brain. Once it gains access, it will then impart its evil desires and wishes into the person's reasoning abilities. The spectator witnessing a physical fight who in a frenzied response keeps shouting, "Kill him, and kill him" is in fact expressing the desire of the demon who is manipulating that person's thoughts. An angry mob is nothing more than a cluster of demons gathered around people who don't have a working personal relationship with God. If you happen to be among the crowd, you will have an uphill battle struggling against the hoards of demonic clusters converged on the event to not get sucked into such demonic behavior.

Whenever a group of people become upset or angry, they attract the attention of multiple demons. While waiting at the airport boarding gate for my flight I have encountered on more than one occasion that dreaded announcement that the departure time has been delayed for two hours or more. I watched as fellow passengers upset by the news would go up to the attendant and begin to complain and get angry. Like a cancer, angry feelings began to infect the rest of us and before you knew it, just about everyone developed angry feelings. I watched trivial arguments break out between couples flying together. I saw how frustrated angry passengers vented their anger at the gate attendant or the nearby concession stand operator. At the core of all of this is a cluster of demons that were infusing negative angry thoughts into an environment charged with disappointment, frustration, and irritability.

Be careful not to bring that attitude home with you because if you do, chances are you have tapped into the energy of a cluster of demons all too eager to follow you home. When you are surrounded by a bunch of disgruntled and/or negative people, immediately vacate the area and go somewhere else so that their negativity doesn't infect you. If you can't get away then divert your attention and energy away from the grumbling at hand. Take out a book, commune with God, make a list of all the blessings in your life, listen to music if you can. Point is, create a mental distraction so that you don't get sucked into the vibrational pattern of a whole bunch of demons. Think of it as a twister. The cluster of demons converging on a bunch of disgruntled people is the funnel cloud. Growing feelings of anger and hostility just sucks the life right out of anything in its path. If you get too close to a twister then you risk getting pulled into the funnel cloud. Keep your distance!!!!

Please don't get at angry at God either. No matter how horrible or tragic a circumstance can be, don't wonder, "How could a loving God have done this"? The reality is that God didn't. God is incapable of evil. It is Satan who is evil and influences man to create and carry out horrific man–made acts of evil against all living creatures. I am always amazed when I see people shaking their fists towards the sky and cursing God for tragedies that Satan orchestrated.

When you get angry at God you will literally grab the attention of nearby demons because you are expressing their deepest hateful feelings about God. Like attracts like. It is a quick way to have a cluster of demons shadow you around for a while hoping for and encouraging more of the same. Godless acts of evil are just that… "God–less"; or without God. When weather tragedies strike, it is easy to forget that we and not God have tampered with the earth through our own interventions. Green house gases, nuclear underground testing, bio–weaponry, pollution, and mass destruction of our eco–forests have created climatic changes drastically altering our weather patterns. God created the earth in perfect balance. God allows tragedies partly because of our free will to choose to commit them and mostly to help us understand and grow in faith through trials and to trust in

Him. Instead of being angry, look for God in the aftermath. He is already there waiting for you to reach out to Him.

Controlling Anger

Anger by far is one of the most destructive emotions we can harbor. It gives off such powerful negative energy that demons come running when they sense this emotion. Once around you they will attempt to plant trigger thoughts in your head that only serve to escalate the feeling of anger.

Plan of Action

1. The first thing you need to do is discern the thoughts going through your head. Sort out fact from conjecture. Take a moment to stop when you feel yourself getting angry. Pause and take a few deep breaths. By doing this you are bringing more oxygen into your brain which helps with clarity. When we get angry we tend to say things, especially hurtful things without thinking. Taking this pause allows the Holy Spirit to intervene as a "voice" in your head helping you gain perspective, and think rationally again. Listen to that inner voice of reason. This makes the demons incredibly mad where they will try to get the other person even more fired up so as to draw you back in to the argument. Don't take the bait!

2. Ask for heavenly assistance to help you deal with the matter in a calm, rational, and godly manner. Remember that demons are always present when anger is expressed. Call on your guardian angel to intervene and fight the demonic influences with you. Everyone has a guardian angel around them 24/7 waiting to assist you so don't be shy and ask for their help. Don't allow yourself to get angry and start shouting at the other person, or even at the demons. By doing so you are giving the demons

exactly what they want; your attention and energy. Pray silently for guidance and self-control instead of obsessing about how angry you feel.

3. Say a prayer of understanding and love, silent or out loud, for the one who is or has offended you. Don't forget that the evil ones will use anyone to attack you, even your closest friends. Anger that is controlled by demons will express itself with terribly hurtful words that cause great emotional pain long after the argument has ended. Don't let a demon cause emotional heartache to your dearest friends or family members through your unchecked anger. When we offer up a heartfelt prayer for someone else we are basically sending them a pearl of unconditional love. It is impossible to be both severely angry and in a state of heartfelt prayer simultaneously. When you begin to pray in earnest, you immediately cut off all "fuel" that the demons can throw on the "fire" (argument). Sincere prayer brings us close to God and sends away the demons screaming in disgust.

4. Acknowledge a spiritual victory. When you get so angry that you want to say or do something extremely rash but you choose not to, that is a huge victory. Say for instance that your brain screams, "Smack him in the face", but an inner voice says, "Walk away", and you leave the confrontation without acting on that impulse, then good battled evil, and evil lost. Quite literally a demon whispered for you to physically assault someone and yet your angel or the Holy Spirit advised you to walk away instead, thereby preventing a dangerous, potentially violent altercation from occurring. Not acting on an impulse that causes further harm (emotionally or physically) is the perfect way to send a clear signal to the demons that good is stronger than evil.

5. Even if you walk away, never go to bed angry. If you do, demons will be able to infiltrate your subconscious while you sleep. If you ever went to bed mad, woke up even angrier at the person, and then stewed about it all day, chances are the demon or demons intensified those feelings while you slept! Ephesians 4:26 warns against this very thing, "In your anger do not sin. Do not let the sun go down while you are still angry, and do not give the devil a foothold."

No matter how justified your anger may seem, make your last waking thoughts be about all things heavenly. Read something spiritual right before going to bed. It won't be easy at first to ignore your anger but keep in mind you are in the middle of a spiritual battle for your soul. You are wrestling against absolute evil spirit beings whose only mission is to see you self-destruct. Fight off the devilish temptation to let your anger fester. By doing so, you will be able to claim a small victory in this spiritual war. When you are feeling angry, pinpointing rationally, calmly, and objectively, the cause of the misunderstanding is the last thing you want to do, yet by doing so, you are actually developing godly character and growing spiritually. Take to heart the rules for holy living in Colossians 3:8, "But now you must rid yourselves of all such things as these: anger, rage, malice, slander, and filthy language from your lips."

Being Held Hostage By Fear

Fear acts like a homing beacon for demons. Next to anger, fear is another powerful emotion that demons have an insatiable appetite for. Fear draws in multiple demons. Demons that specialize and are experts in their respective fields such as anxiety, worry, suspicion, self-doubt, and depression to name a few, always band together and come as a cluster to torment some poor soul caught up in the emotion of fear. A constant state of fear is an open invitation for demons to come barging in and set up a command post in your head. Once inside, they manage to get you to replace truth with irrational thoughts which creates a hesitancy and/or resistance to move past the fear because of the doubt they planted. The doubt originated with them and not you.

The fear of people finding out who you really are or what you have done in the past causes isolation. We were born as interactive beings because interacting with people teaches us godly virtues and warns of evil principles. The fear of demons that has you over analyzing every negative thing in your life keeps you from fully enjoying life. Fear forgets that while we all have demons around us, we also have angels surrounding us too with a ratio of 2:1 with the odds in our favor. Dwelling on what is wrong in our life creates a tendency to fixate on the negative aspects of our life. This in turn sets us up with a fear of being a failure in general. Demons are all too eager to agree that you are a failure at life and will whisper those thoughts into your subconscious if you don't try to address the fear.

Fear that is based on a wrong assumption and is irrational draws a cluster of demons into your space. Becoming frozen with fear only provides demons with food that sustains them to hang around even longer. We can waste so much time justifying why the irrational fear prevents us from doing something with a million excuses that prevent us from taking the first step. The reality is that we could have accomplished that task in half the time we wasted on rationalizing why we couldn't do it.

When Fear Dominates Your Thoughts — Confusion Dictates Your Words

Jesus himself told us, "Peace I leave with you; my peace I give you. I do not give to you as the world gives. Do not let your hearts be troubled and do not be afraid", John 14:28 (NIV). Our Savior himself asks us to not be fearful of anything but to accept his freely offered serenity. Trust Jesus' plan for your life. Accepting Jesus' promises for your life will cause you so much less stress and anxiety over the "unknowns". Jesus is in control and not the demons of fear. Don't let demonically planted fears frighten you away from God. God never carelessly throws us into any situation. Trials that come our way are only allowed when God feels we have whatever it takes to endure and grow in character, no matter how desperate the situation presents itself. Our God supplies the courage we will need to endure the hardship at hand.

Our obsessive need to control every aspect of our lives creates immense stress because the demons have convinced you that you can't trust anyone but yourself to script your life. Stop thinking that it is you that has to figure everything out. Remove yourself from the center of the universe and put God back there instead. If God stepped in every time and stopped the circumstance that caused us to be afraid, how would we ever be able to develop trust, courage, faith, and acceptance? So stop struggling with fear no matter how justified you feel it is. Let go and let God. II Timothy 1:7 says, "For God has not given us a spirit of fear, but a spirit of power, of love and self-discipline."

Overriding the Demons of Fear

As soon as you notice yourself becoming fearful try to let go of the fear by calming yourself down. Calming yourself stops the stream of continued fearful thoughts being put there by either a demon or a cluster of demons. By doing this you are allowing the light of the Holy Spirit to squeeze in past the fortress of fear and bring clarity back to the circumstance at hand. You will be able to see the situation in a new light. View the object of your fear as a teaching opportunity for spiritual growth. Embrace this chance with total trust that God is directing your life and watch the demons scatter like a bunch of marbles dropped on the floor. Instead of being fearful over not knowing what is around the corner for your life, be excited over the opportunities that await your discovery.

Stop obsessing over the "hows". "How could I of have let this happen? How am I supposed to change my behavior, life, career, etc.? How am I going to get by?"

The "how's" are demonic instruments of fear designed to promote undue anxiety and fear within you deliberately so that you won't trust in God's plan for your life. If left unchecked, it will give birth to procrastination which basically means that you are frozen with fear but deny that fact by justifications (excuses) of why you can't move forward. Procrastination feels comfortable because it nurtures and cuddles fear through inaction. The problem is that this "state" will be exploited by any and all demons surrounding you and applied by them to other areas of your life, in particular your spiritual life! God is the God of perfect love. Satan is the god of fear. I John 4:18–19 tells us, "There is no fear in love. But perfect love casts out fear, because fear has to do with punishment. The one who fears is not made perfect in love. We love because He (God) first loved us."

Phrases that are Praises to a Demonic Cluster
When we speak we send out for all to hear what we are

thinking. Even when you are alone, whatever you say out loud is heard by both heavenly beings and the evil ones that are nearby. All too often we carelessly toss out expletives (swear words) without reflecting on the power those words convey. Using the Lord's name in vain (like screaming out "Jesus Christ" in anger) with such negatively charged emotions is the equivalent of a defiant demonic "halleluiah". Seemingly simple words or phrases we use to "let off steam" that disrespect heaven in any way is music to a demon's ear. I am not saying that using such phrases means that a cluster of demons will attack you, but it sure will draw them into your space. Getting rid of one demonic influence in your life is challenging enough so why would you want to increase that challenge tenfold by using such expressions and attracting a cluster? No matter how "devout" a person may seem, if they have a "potty mouth" (foul mouth), they will probably have their own demonic entourage following them around where ever they go. James 1:26 (KJV) says it succinctly, "If any man among you seems to be religious and bridles not his tongue, but deceives his own heart, this man's religion is in vain".

Top Five Expressions that Act Like a Dog Whistle Summoning the Hounds of Hell

1. **"God damn it"**. In this phrase you are directly asking that the Creator of the Universe to curse someone or something into hell forever. It is said in an atmosphere of anger where no love is present, only hate. If you derive some sort of satisfaction from using that expression, that satisfaction means you are under the influence of demonic thought tampering. If saying it gives you a sense of power, you are tapped into the mindset of demons. To a demon this selfish unholy request means that you have the audacity to ask God to commit an evil act on your command. In essence you are ordering God to do your

dirty work!

2. **"Why don't you just drop dead"**. By saying this you are actually pronouncing a form of a curse on someone else because you are wishing for them to die. When I was in school I was constantly bullied. There was always a group of girls who would publicly humiliate me and then tell me to drop dead. As I tried to walk away I would either trip in my nervousness or drop my books. That made them cackle in delight and hurl even more insults my way such as "loser" or "moron". To actually feel delight in someone else's pain is a "character trait" of demons. To laugh at someone's misfortune after telling them to drop dead is an obvious tell– tale sign that they are under the influence of a cluster of demons. Having "friends" or people support or encourage such behavior means there is a cluster of demons at work within that group.

3. **"I swear to God"**. This expression means that you are making an unbreakable vow in front of God regarding your innocence. Jesus himself warned against swearing to God in Matthew 5:33–37, "Again you have heard that it was said to the people long ago, do not break your oath, but keep oaths you have made to the Lord. But I tell you, do not swear at all: either by heaven, for it is God's throne; or by the earth, for it is his footstool; or by Jerusalem for it is the city of the Great King. And do not swear by your head, for you cannot make even one hair white or black. Simply let your 'yes' be 'yes' and your 'no', 'no'; anything beyond this comes from the evil one."

To use this expression to hide behind a false innocence is disgusting. Not only are you lying but you are manipulating the other person's trust by getting them to believe that God is vouching for your innocence. This expression is a favorite of demons everywhere.

4. **"Hocus Pocus"**. Mainly this phrase is used in magic tricks but every now and then I hear it when someone says something to the effect, "There is a lot of "hocus pocus" going on there". No Catholic should ever use this phrase as it is a derogatory corruption referring to the Eucharist; "Hoc Est Corpus" or "This is my body". Protestants back in the Middle Ages used this corrupted term to mock the Holy Eucharist celebration of the Mass. They would hurl this insult not only at clergy but also Catholic lay people on their way to Mass.

5.

6. **"Kiss my ass"**. I saved this expression for last because it is especially vulgar. Sadly it is such a common expression in our society today spoken to show defiance. It is better known to Satanists everywhere as the "oscularum infame" or kiss of shame. During the traditional black mass this was considered a symbolic requisite towards earthly success. Participants would literally kiss the bare behind of the devil (usually the high priest conducting the mass). Nothing gets a cluster of demons charging headlong towards somebody faster than using excerpts from the satanic mass.

Safety Protocols of Protection From Demonic Clusters:

1. I recommend as a precaution to not bringing home any demonic clusters that you do the following. Keep some holy water and blessed salt in your vehicle. I also always carry a small vial of holy water in my pocket. Whenever I find myself in an environment where there is a lot of tension, I discreetly make the sign of the cross on my

forehead with holy water. Before getting into my truck I will use a spray bottle filled with holy water and give a few squirts inside before stepping in. If I feel that I have been around a cluster of demons I will place a ring of blessed salt around the exterior of my truck before entering so as not to allow them access inside my vehicle. If I know that someone will enter my house that I feel has a negative influence tailing them I will spray each room with holy water. I always add a few drops of holy water to any water I use to make and serve as a beverage to such a guest and a few grains of blessed salt in the salt shaker add an extra measure of protection. Do this without the person's knowledge of course.

2. Pray! Pray for protection. Pray that St. Michael the Archangel be by your side and ward off any demons attempting to follow you home. Pray to the Blessed Mother for protection. Say the rosary or at least a Hail Mary. Pray, pray, pray! I made up a saying that I will share with you and it is great advice to remember. "For all the things out there in this world that can kill you, overdosing on prayer isn't one of them!"

3. Leave all negative thoughts and emotions at the door before entering your home. Force yourself to over ride such negative feelings and emotions with reflecting on a moment of joy you experienced in the past. Think of a "warm fuzzy" or whatever it takes to stop the stream of negative thoughts before walking through the door. Sometimes I will sit an extra five minutes in my truck listening to music I know lifts my mood rather than bringing that negativity inside my home. Such a heavy or negative feeling that comes on after you have left home may indicate that a cluster of demons are shadowing you. Don't allow that in your house! Shake off that mood

before entering.

My friend once told me a cute saying she read off someone's bumper sticker. I think I will leave you with that quote. "When Satan knocks on your door, have Jesus answer it for you."

"And the God of all grace, who called you to his eternal glory in Christ, after you have suffered a little while, will himself restore you and make you strong, firm and steadfast. To him be the power forever and ever. Amen." I Peter 5:10–11.

Chapter 9

Occult Involvement: Dancing with Demons

If you are looking for a sure fire way to attract and have a demon or a cluster of demons attach themselves to you, dabble in the occult. Many people wrongly assume that as long as they don't practice witchcraft or worship the devil they will be safe. Anything that involves the spirit realm or predicting the future is opening the door to evil. Thanks to the ever increasingly popular TV shows about the spirit world and ghost hunting shows, our teens are being drawn by this pied piper to blindly follow and explore the spirit realm out of curiosity. Individuals who experiment with the occult often dabble in methods without fully understanding the ramifications, or comprehending the powers they are invoking. There is a wealth of metaphysical books out there that say we all have "spirit guides" just waiting for us to contact them for our personal spiritual enlightenment. I can say truthfully and also from painful firsthand experience, these "spirits" or "spirit guides" that are attracted to our curiosity are almost always demons.

The guaranteed way to protect yourself from demonic infestation is to prevent them from attaching themselves to you to begin with. Don't dabble in the occult; don't play around with the Ouija board or read books on such topics "just to be informed". Don't ask for "signs" of the spirit world to reveal itself to you. Don't engage in the "I dare you" game of having someone prove that they aren't afraid of spirits by having that person do something scary like walk alone through a cemetery at night. Demons don't behave like humans. Devoid of any mercy, they are extremely dangerous and more powerful than you. It is much easier to attract and have a demon follow you home than it is to get rid of it once it takes up residence in your life.

Don't Attempt to Put Out the Fires of Hell Armed Only With a Kitchen Fire Extinguisher!

I am receiving an alarming number of requests for help in demonic haunting by Christians with no apparent occult involvement. They are experiencing similar if not identical demonic issues as those who directly summoned a demon into their life despite their devout faith. What I am finding is that these "Christians" plagued by an upper level demon actually invited the thing into their life unknowingly through arrogance disguised as zealousness. These are well intentioned people who read a book or two on demonology and then feel "qualified" to rescue someone plagued by demonic activity. That is as dangerous as a teenager who just got his learner permit to drive, getting behind the wheel of an eighteen wheeler and driving that tractor trailer rig through the narrow streets of New York City while texting on his phone at the same time! They have a sense of invincibility because they feel they will harness the power of Jesus is their undoing. Ironically it is their innocence of not fully comprehending the evil they are taking on that is so attractive to a demon.

A demon cannot resist the temptation to re–direct its attention onto the destruction of innocence, especially if it involves the chance of shaking the foundations of that person's faith. I have witnessed more than a few Christians ride off to battle telling me that in the name of Jesus they can cast out a demon. I have seen them return terrified, now tormented by the very demon they wanted to banish, and questioning why Jesus failed to cast out the demon in the person they were trying to help. It wasn't Jesus who failed. These individuals failed to respect the power they were up against, and failed to realize that any unresolved or unconfessed sin(s) can and will be used against them because that is the opening the demon seeks out in order to gain a foothold in that person's life. Demons can't "connect" with goodness, but they will connect with evil no matter how miniscule. If you have done anything to offend God, trust me, it acts as a GPS tracking device to a demon. The sacrament of confession is mandatory before taking part in ANY sort of direct spiritual warfare! One has to check their emotions at the door before engaging any demon and enter with a spirit of humility, have no unconfessed sins that the demons can "sniff" out, be fortified with the Eucharist, and remember that they aren't vested with the same authority by God or the church as a priest.

A lay person can never take the place of a priest in engaging demons!! No action is better than the wrong action in these matters. Leave the "front line fighting" to the experts in the field. The reason why demons fear priests is because the Catholic Church is the Holy Apostolic Church of Jesus. In

Luke 10 Jesus appoints seventy disciples to go out two by two to every city to announce his coming there. These seventy disciples came back and were really joyful that demons were subject to them through Jesus' name. In verse 19 Jesus says, "Behold, I give unto you the power to tread on serpents and scorpions, and over all the power of the enemy (Satan): and nothing shall by any means hurt you." Jesus didn't give that authority to the multitudes of people he preached to. He appointed seventy disciples and gave them that authority. Men who become Catholic priests are in a sense "appointed" by Jesus to do his work which includes spiritual warfare.

Jesus also called the apostle Peter the "rock" and gave him the "keys to the kingdom" and told him that upon this "rock" he would build his church. Jesus invested the authority to minister to the world and to cast out demons to the apostles. Priests today are the spiritual descendants of the apostles of Jesus and have this authority to cast out demons, and demons fear this power because they know the Catholic Church is the true church of God!!

Having been a Protestant most of my adult life I have witnessed their interventions for demonic issues and I have not seen them to be successful in true demonic haunting. I am excluding those people convinced they are possessed by the demon of fear, anger, etc. who become "healed" after being prayed over. Generally in those situations it was more of an emotional healing stemming from feelings as opposed to a true demonic possession. I am seeing an alarming trend by Catholics and non-Catholics to use the strategies outlined for priests by books written by exorcists, and use them incorrectly. To not follow any instruction to the letter of the law only provokes the demon not because of the fear of you, but because of the audacity of a mere mortal to attempt to take on a "superior" spirit being. You then not only announce your presence to this demon but you offer it up a challenge to take you on so as to break your spirit and ruin your soul. Demons do fear priests that know how to cast them out. Except for a few rare exceptions, demons do not fear nor respect lay people. Never forget that you are their "bread and butter". They work solely for the reward of destruction and ruin of your soul!

Every Time Someone Engages a Demon There Will Be Repercussions, Period!!

I cannot state this any clearer or succinctly. Attempting to rid a home or individual by a lay person of a demon infuriates the demon. They will throw all sorts of negativity your way as a result to "put you in your place" and "show you who is boss". People who have engaged a demon without the proper experience and training will inadvertently feel the ramifications of their act. Feelings of depression, hopelessness, irritability, fatigue, and a general sense of negativity is common. Nightmares, freak accidents, trials of all sorts, problems at home or work, physical illness, and a sense of not feeling close to God are very common after such an encounter. In worse case scenarios demonic infestation of the home of the intervener can take place. If you really want to help someone with demonic issues, the most effective weapon against a demon is prayer. Pray diligently for the person afflicted. Ask the Blessed Mother to send her angels to the afflicted person. Be a support and prayer warrior. Leave the heroics up to the "special forces". Chapter ten will discuss in detail the strategies and weapons you need to defend yourself from the evil ones.

Addiction to Prediction

Horoscopes, or as I like to spell it, "horror–scopes", are extremely popular in our society. Just about every newspaper carries a daily horoscope. Horoscopes are predictions of what will happen in your life based on planetary alignments. People get addicted to astrology and reading horoscopes daily to plan their days according to what is "projected" for their particular "star sign". Demons cannot "predict" the future. That is why they orchestrate horoscopes to be so vague in nature that it applies to anyone and everyone regardless of their "sign". Following horoscopes shifts the focus off from trusting God to provide for our needs and growth. It essentially places that trust into the hands of demons that will lure you away from God with empty promises based on a lie. The danger here is that this is a "baby step" (curiosity to learn more) into exploring deeper more sinister realms of the occult where the individual will have direct contact with a demon. Believing that your character is etched in stone because of the sign you were born under basically sabotages any attempts to overcome your character defects because you were "born that way". As a teenager I used to do horoscopes and palm readings for my public high school teachers so as to "bribe" them into giving me better grades. The human curiosity factor of wanting to know what the future held meant that I was very successful in this endeavor.

Portals

A portal is a gateway and direct opening into the spirit world. Although the spirit world and physical world co-exist, they run parallel to each other. God in His perfect wisdom placed a veil between the two worlds so that you and I can concentrate in this physical life on developing godly traits based on faith, trust, and God's word. God also knows that as humans it would be too much of a burden to fully comprehend how the spiritual realm operates. Imagine if everyone could all of the time see angels and demons meander around us? Every time you would see a violent street gang, you would also see a cluster of the most vile and monstrous demons surrounding them. Life would become too frightening to live.

There are opportunities for the two worlds to intersect via a portal. Portals are demonic creations designed to rip holes in this veil of separation. Portals are always demonic, despite their initial benign appearance. They are openings that allow "spirits" (demons) to come and go as *they* please. Generally they are activated by people who have participated in rituals or practices designed specifically to open them and attract "spirits". They can be specific symbols to summon entities drawn on a wall or floor by individuals who practice black magic or witchcraft expecting the entity to grant them supernatural powers. Or it can be the result of direct spirit communications such as through the Ouija Board, séances, pendulums, Tarot or psychic readings, automatic writing, table tipping, channeling or ghost hunting. These are some of the preferred methods that welcome sinister upper level demons into a person's life.

Such evil energy is simply not found in ordinary people's homes. People who have such evil spirits in their home have usually participated either knowingly or unknowingly in a summoning ritual (opened up a portal). In rare cases some unfortunate people have moved into homes where the previous residents had practiced those dark portal rituals. Upper level demons are very powerful and unmistakable when they "infest" a location.

Signs of Demonic Manifestation (When No Logical Explanations Exist) Include but Aren't Limited to:
- Injuring or killing of the family pet(s)

- Pets displaying extremely fearful behaviors at nothing and for no apparent reason such as barking, growling, hissing , hiding while staring at some unseen presence

- Black shadowy forms drifting around the home

- Personal objects such as keys, wallet, eye glasses disappearing and reappearing in strange places where you know you didn't leave them

- Moving heavy furniture or appliances

- Raspy growling, or hissing noises not made by an animal

- A sinister menacing deep low voice yelling threats such as, "GET OUT!" or something like "You're gonna die!"

- Foul and putrid smells

- Loud knocks or bangs

- Mechanical or electrical malfunctions

- Physical attacks such as unexplained scratches or bruising on the body particularly in hard to reach places such as the back

- An overwhelming sense of fear and darkness when entering the location

- Unexplained dark behavioral changes in a family member or friend

- Physical illnesses that have no medical explanation

Once a portal doorway is opened, they don't shut by themselves. It is much easier to open a portal than it is to close one. An open portal allows any "passing by" evil spirit entry into this realm. You cannot control or regulate who or what comes through. If you do shut a portal doorway without banishing back the demon that came through it, you risk "trapping" that demon in that particular space or location. I use the word "trap" loosely because the demon sees this as a limitless golden opportunity to torment all unsuspecting individuals who live and visit in the home with a portal it would normally not have had access to. If you or someone you know has opened a portal door, it is essential that you or they find someone qualified to close the portal door. Don't attempt to do it yourself if you don't know how to do so. That only ends up provoking the evil entity that has crossed into the physical realm and it will retaliate against you. My first suggestion is to always seek out the counsel of a priest familiar with spiritual warfare and the occult to help in these matters.

Messing around with a Ouija Board or holding a séance in a home directly attracts and invites the spirit realm into your home. It is always a bad idea to invite "ghosts" to communicate with you. There are some very foolish people out there who actually go out looking for ghosts just to invite them home for some of the dumbest reasons ranging from wanting company to wanting notoriety for living in a haunted home. Demons view these individuals who practice this as unsuspecting idiots trying to contact them. They will "toy" with such people by pretending to be their dearly departed loved one just to gain their trust and get them addicted to "talking" to spirits via the spirit board (Ouija Board). Demons are tricksters and will say anything to "hook" the person so as to elicit strong emotional energetic reactions which demons feed on. From there demons will attempt (under the guise of some dearly beloved departed soul) to lure these people into trying their hand (no pun intended) at automatic writing, or worse yet, channeling. Automatic writing is when you invite a spirit to move the pen you are holding to write something (a direct statement from the spirit) on the paper in front of you. Channeling is when you allow a spirit to communicate through your body. Both are forms of temporary possessions by "spirits" which are actually demons in disguise.

It has been my experience as a paranormal investigator to have witnessed earthbound human spirits attempt communication through manipulation of electronic devices, sudden unexplainable knocks or bangs, or by apparition. I have found that there is no great desire for deceased "human" spirits to enter a body to communicate with the living. People when they die generally "cross over" to the other side or realm. That means that they go to heaven, purgatory, or worst case scenario, hell. Think of it; why would your recently deceased mom want to inhabit the body of an imperfect and flawed human anyway to tell you she is OK, when she could have a new spirit body free of all physical defects and be in heaven talking to the Blessed Mother about you? The only creatures that lust for such an experience are demons that have never incarnated as human beings. Allowing such forms of spirit communication acts as a "test drive" for a demon to get a "feel" of the body that it wants to eventually take ownership of.

Channeling, automatic writing, Ouija Boards, and séances involve a form of temporary possession. Those who practice this art will try to convince you that they are only allowing beings of pure light to enter their body. The reality is that you don't have concrete proof that whoever is communicating through someone is in fact that deceased person or enlightened "spirit guide". Think of it as just as dangerous as meeting a stranger in human form in a dark alley where you have no idea of their intent. You shouldn't be walking alone down a dark alley in the first place. How many "good Samaritans" do you think lurk in such locales anyway? Stay away from direct or indirect spirit communication.

"It's Only a Kid's Game"

Many times people overlook the dangers associated with certain children's games because of the false assumption that children aren't "serious" or "aware" of what they are playing. Demons are aggressive and will take advantage of innocence just as quickly as they will arrogance. An age old child's game that I played as a kid is making a comeback due to the movie industry's utilization of it in their horror flicks. The game is called, "Bloody Mary". Here one child or a group of children dares another child to stand in front of a mirror in total darkness and call out "Bloody Mary" three to thirteen times in order to see if they can summon the "ghost" of a murdered child. The "rules" state that if this ghost appears then someone in the family of child who summoned it will die. Usually one prankster in the group yells out "BOO!" during this dare to really scare the child doing the summoning.

This is not a game! It is known as "skrying" in witchcraft circles where an individual looks into a mirror (usually only by candlelight) and calls out an entity by name to summon forth that "deity" (demon in disguise). The child being "dared" reeks of fear which acts as an aphrodisiac to a demon. If the child actually entertains thoughts that he or she could be successful in seeing bloody Mary in the mirror, it acts as an invitation to demons to attach themselves to the child. Sadly if an attachment occurs, the child begins to have night terrors and complain of "monsters" coming at night, but the parents unaware of the Bloody Mary game dismiss the child's fears as simply a common childhood phase. Unlike other children's games where you can go back and restart the game, there are no "do–overs" when dealing with demons! Every interaction whether it is direct or indirect with a demon will have repercussions. When someone places a "call" to a demon (intentionally or unintentionally), the demon never puts that person on hold, but answers after the first "ring". They don't care how old you are. Demons are equal opportunity tormentors that don't discriminate based on age, gender, race, or color.

The Goth Movement:
A Demonic Siren Luring Our Teens to Crash Upon the Rocks

You have seen the teens: the ones dressed in all black clothing with multiple piercings and tattoos all over their body, black fingernail polish, dyed black hair, torn fishnet stockings, and spiked collars or wrist bands. They listen to heavy punkish metal songs where the lead singer screams in a distorted low gravely growl like tone which attempts to simulate a demonic voice. Bands are aptly named such as: "Christian Death", "The Damned", "Inkubus Sukkubus", "The Lords of the New Church", "Nosferatu", "Southern Death Cult", "Screaming Dead", "Two Witches", and "45 Grave" to name a few; all promote anti Christian, pro-demon rhetoric in their lyrics.

Demons infiltrate the subconscious of such teens through the lyrics and get them to do their bidding subliminally. Such subliminal exposure to extremely negative energy through music generated by demonic infiltration will open up these teens to embrace a soft core form of Satanism. They display jewelry and clothing with obvious symbols used in hard core Satanism. Through the lyrics they familiarize themselves with the names and functions of specific demons. These teens progress from well behaved pleasant adolescents to disrespectful, sarcastic moody, rude, sullen, anti–establishment and anti–religious defiant individuals. Whenever I see hard core "Goth–heads" I sense strong demonic attachments around them. These teens are only a thin fine line away from demonic possession because as they embrace this "cult" many willingly desire to "commune" with particular demons that promise revenge on those who wronged them or don't approve of their lifestyle.

The teen years are plagued by hormonal fluctuations which create wide range negative and defiant mood swings. Teenage anger is very powerful negative energy that is harnessed and manipulated by demonic entities to promote more such energy. Demons who "feed" on this energy turn the Goth teens into virtual power plants producing more of the same negative energy. By eliciting strong emotional reactions through lyrics and adrenaline pumping heavy metal tunes, demons attach themselves like a blood sucking parasite to their victims. These teens are at great risk for severe demonic infestation and possible demonic possession.

Romanizing demonic possession through lyrics to rebellious teens risks the teen offering up their souls out of parental defiance without being aware of the eternal ramifications of such a stupid act. Wherever these teenagers go, the demons attached to them follow, bringing discontentment, strife, and angry confrontations with them. It is no surprise that in the homes of these Goth followers there are a lot of family arguments as a result of their "lifestyle". Demons can't resist creating an environment of chaos of those they have attached themselves to.

Ghost Hunting:
Who is Hunting Who?

I can't be clear enough when it comes to warning people about the dangers of chasing after the spirit world. Numerous TV reality shows about ghost hunters have sprung up in the last five years and have attracted a big following of ghost hunter wanna–be's. Ghost hunting is becoming a very popular hobby fueled by all the wrong motivations to take up such an activity. The main motivation seems to be curiosity. As a paranormal investigator myself, I cringe whenever someone tells me how exciting it must be to "see" a ghost. I don't need to see or experience a ghost. I do it to help people afflicted with paranormal activity. I look for scientific explanations first and with all the high tech equipment I have, most times the source of the "paranormal" activity is found to be of physical and not spiritual origins.

With my personal background in the occult, I am aware of signs that indicate demonic presences. I have a Master's degree in counseling which not only helps in dealing with people's fears, but also helps me determine if the individual might be suffering from an organic (non-spiritual) form of mental illness. People who call me are frightened, desperate, and begging for help to resolve the issue. My main motivation is to help them resolve their paranormal issue(s). It is not "exciting" when I see the look of terror on the faces of people dealing with such presences in their life. Since my soul was rescued from the clutches of a demon by the Blessed Mother, I seize this second chance at redemption to make restitution to God for my most grievous sins. My acts of contrition include helping others out of the same hell I once was in. This is my reason for being a paranormal investigator with a specialty of demonology.

For the most part, demons are attracted to locations were violent crimes took place. This includes homes where murders occurred. They won't think twice to impersonate the murdered person just to gain the trust of unsuspecting ghost hunters or the individuals residing in that location. Oftentimes demons also impersonate the "spirit" of a dead child. Because the death of a child is always untimely, their guardian angel personally escorts them safely up to heaven. Children don't linger in torment alone in limbo here on earth for centuries. Think about it. A loving God would not subject some innocent child to such a nightmare of eternal suffering and isolation! Demons however will use this ploy because it "pulls on the heart strings" of many people who in turn become far too eager to engage with such a "spirit" because they want to comfort the "child" who must be lonely and lost. No one likes to see a child suffer, but the reality is that demons are using this human vulnerability to attach themselves to an individual.

Far too many "ghost hunters" are not only terribly ignorant of how to protect themselves from evil, but aren't even aware of how easily something can follow them home. Demons thrive in an environment of habitual sin. Demons have a much easier time accessing the minds of individuals who don't have a close personal relationship with God. I don't care how many non-religious people engage in this type of paranormal investigation activity; you can't believe in demons and then not believe in God. For those out there who believe in demons and not God, when they go on a paranormal investigation, they are riding into a spiritual battle totally unarmed! They are going to bring their "work" home with them. Wanting to make deliberate contact with a ghost is opening up a portal gateway where you can't decide who comes through and who doesn't. It's a game of Russian roulette for your soul. More times than not, it is a demon and not a ghost that will attach themselves to the investigator.

Demonic Imprinting

Whenever a person is heavily involved in the occult, when they encounter a demon, they will be "imprinted" by that demon, (I talked about this in chapter five, but I feel it is important to reiterate this significant point). That demonic encounter registers in every cell of that person's body. Demons are pure spirit comprised of energy and although we are organic matter, our body is governed by electrical impulses emitting energy fields. If a demonic energy comes in contact with human energy (particularly in the brain), there is an exchange of electrical impulses. The residue of that encounter becomes imprinted in the memory of the cells in the brain. Since thoughts and feelings are the result of hundreds of millions of electrical firings within the cells of our brain, direct communication with demons, be it from trying to engage them verbally or allowing them to "speak through" you will leave a demonic "residue". This residue when it comes into contact with "trigger" objects, thoughts, or actions, will re–awaken latent thoughts, feelings, and memories "imprinted" during the electrical impulse exchange with a demonic force.

Demonic triggers are designed to reconstitute desires to reengage in occult practices. These triggers promise a euphoric "high" that is very hard to resist. Unfortunately, once you are imprinted, it will last your lifetime. Triggers can appear decades after you have renounced all occult involvement, where they are apt to blindside you. Triggers vary from individual to individual. I myself fell victim to a demonic trigger just last year that caught me completely by surprise. Those of us who have been heavily involved in the occult must constantly be on guard for such 'attacks" and must reach out to someone they trust for support and guidance when faced with a trigger. We must also stay very close to God in our daily walk. Demons will try to infuse thoughts of isolation through guilt and shame deliberately just so you don't reach out when it is critical to do so. Remember the demonic code of "divide and conquer" is designed so that you remain isolated from the Holy Spirit working through another individual.

The "Athame":
My Personal Story of an Experience with a Demonic Trigger Object

After a perfect day of sightseeing while on vacation, I was walking back to my hotel. As I reflected on the blessings of my life, something unusual on the ground caught my attention. It was a plastic dagger that vaguely seemed familiar. I bent down to pick it up. The moment my fingers came in contact with it, instinctively I knew it to resemble an athame or ceremonial dagger used in ritual magic. My conscious immediately went into high alert protesting against this sudden surge of desire that came from deep within my brain. "Surely there can't be any harm in holding a simple child's toy, after all it is impotent and cannot bring forth or conjure up a dust devil, never mind a demon" was my rationale. What I didn't realize was that this seemingly harmless piece of molded plastic was a demonic trigger object that would attempt to seduce me back into my old occult ways subconsciously.

As soon as I grasped the dagger with my right hand my mind was flooded with memories of the days when I practiced the black arts. This was demonic imprinting at work. As I waved the wand in once familiar intricate ceremonial patterns I felt euphoric. It was as if my brain was functioning on auto–pilot because I wasn't even totally aware of what I was doing. The "rush" of power and invincibility was intoxicating. It was as if my brain had not only split in two but was at war with each other. One half saying, "Go on and bask in those memories and feel the power", while the other half countering it with, "What are you doing? You don't want to go back to this… remember the pain".

I realized the danger of literally fondling this "thing' but I couldn't throw it back down where I found it. Instead I put it in my coat pocket as a reference guide with the logical conclusion that I will check the local stores to see if this knife came out of some child's Viking play set. Maybe I was just over reacting over a common medieval play toy. Strangely, it felt comforting to know that this object now was mine; it were as if I had reconnected with a long lost friend.

The next day I scoured the surrounding stores trying to duplicate this toy dagger but found no match. I should have thrown it away then but I didn't because I reasoned that it would make a nice prop someday when I lecture on the topic of this book. I met my friend for lunch and while we waited to be served, I brought it up to her attention. I expected a, "that's really neat" response but instead she was full of concern and began to warn me of the dangers of having such a trigger object in my possession. She adamantly encouraged me to throw it away immediately but it was too late… I had formed an unholy attachment to it. By that point I was being "flooded" with desires and longing due to demonic imprinting. That little plastic knife that suspiciously appeared by my feet was a demonic plant to see if I would take the bait which I did. Once I actually touched the "trigger" knife, it re–awoke those latent desires and feelings associated with its use through cell memory. I was unaware of how it was beginning to affect my judgment and even when pointed out by my friend, I couldn't see how it connected to my days of practicing the black arts.

Unable to part with it, my friend saw an opportunity when I left the knife in her backseat and while I was distracted by something else, threw the knife away without me knowing it. She wisely didn't tell me about doing this until we were quite a ways away. Of course I thanked her and said how grateful I was for her intervention but on the inside I immediately began grieving over my lost plastic friend. I tried to convince myself it was for the best but I couldn't help the feelings of intense loss. It was as if someone had cut off my right arm, so attached had I become to it in such a short time.

I was consumed for hours afterwards by a longing for something that I had found unexpectedly and lost so abruptly by what I perceived as a friend's careless toss, even though I asked God to remove all such impure desires associated with this object. The next day I became consumed with feelings of guilt and shame over lusting over such an object. "What a hypocrite I am… here I profess my allegiance to God publically and yet in the dark and secret I desire all things unholy and detestable to God." The intense guilt and shame tried to convince me that I was a failure in God's eyes and that I was evil to the core. Such thoughts of spiritual sabotage are very common in the wake of triggers. Demons attempt to prevent you from reaching out to God by vividly throwing all your past mistakes in your face. It isn't God who is your accuser, it is Satan. Demons try to confuse you into forgetting all the positive changes you have made when turning your life over to God every day. God in His mercy worked through my friend who was able to help me out of the demonic trap I had fallen into. I wanted to isolate myself from her but she knew about demonic triggers and refused to be pushed away by me.

I am so grateful for her tenacity. It had been over 30 years since I had practiced black magic. I was careful on a conscious level to avoid going to any place or engaging in any activity that could cause me to fall into temptation. I was careful not to associate with anyone who was into the occult. Despite my precautions, I failed to take into account how the demonic imprinting I encountered decades earlier would still be a source of demonic infiltration of my mind through the planting of trigger objects. Being opportunists', demons will wait patiently until your guard (vigilance) is down and then place a seemingly harmless trigger in your path hoping that you will take the "bait".

Demonic Possession:
When You Aren't "Yourself"

Since there are books written about demonic possession by priests who are exorcists, I am only going to give you a brief overview of possession. This book is based upon my experiences and is not intended as a complete theological textbook on demonic hostile takeovers. This is a subject that should not be approached lightly. Because "possession" is a careless term that is thrown out there by people unschooled in demonology whenever someone does something evil, I feel it prudent to include some guidelines about the subject. Many in the protestant community will claim a Christian struggling with whatever issue is "possessed" by the demon of fear, anger, jealously, etc. That is simply not how it works.

In the last year alone I have come into contact with two completely possessed people displaying completely different characteristics. One was endowed with eternal youthful looks at a ripe old age, wealth, and minor celebrity status. She loved to wear all black clothing and jewelry and when I shook her hand, her body and hands were as cold as ice despite the warm summer temperature. Her eyes were completely black and I could smell a strong odor of burning sulfur. The other was an unkempt homeless man covered in boils who had angry incoherent conversations with himself. I was on vacation half way across the country. As I passed by him while sightseeing, he looked up at me and said very profound (trying to frighten and intimidate me) things about my ministry he couldn't possibly have known because I hadn't even begun the ministry yet! Then he went back to arguing incoherently with some unseen being next to him.

Actual possession of a person by a demon is extremely rare. It entails the individual willingly handing over their free will and soul to demonic entities for the specific purpose of allowing possession (barring rare exceptions). Demons promise to endow such individuals with supernatural powers if they are granted access to inhabit the body. Of course demons won't tell you the "side effects" the mind and body will endure as a result of such an unholy union. Trying to integrate demonic energy with human energy goes against the laws of nature. It is like trying to blend oil and water together. Demons who possess a person are psychic vampires who feed on the body's vital energies. As a result physical signs of this disharmony are evident.

A Case Study of Possession:
Mark 5:1–20 and Luke 11:24–26.
Jesus encounters a demon possessed man in Gerasenes who races up to him from the tombs as Jesus got out of the boat. This man had to be chained in a cemetery because he was so mentally unstable he was a danger to others. He possessed super human strength to be able to keep breaking the iron chains that bound his hands and feet. He engaged in self-injurious behavior by cutting himself with stones. This

man also possessed knowledge other men didn't, namely he knew Jesus was the Son of God. This poor tortured soul was so full of inner turmoil and anguish that he cried out every night day in utter agony. When Jesus asks the demon's name, they reply "Legion" which meant "many". I encourage you to read the entire account for yourself in the bible. In true demonic possessions it is common for the individual to display super human strength, violent self-injurious behavior, and knowledge of things the person wouldn't have access to otherwise.

Jesus in Luke 11:24–26 warns about the danger that follows post demonic possession. "When an evil spirit comes out of a man, it goes through arid places seeking rest and does not find it. Then it says, 'I will return to the house I left'. When it arrives, it finds the house unoccupied, swept clean, and put in order. Then it goes and takes with it seven other spirits more wicked than itself, and they go and live there. And the final condition of the man is worse than the first."

These are two perfect examples of seeing demonic operation in classic possessions. It shows that a demon can come and go in and out of a possessed person as they please. Possessed people can appear very normal at times and have "crisis" periods where the demon is back. In the original 1970's movie about exorcism, evidence of demonic possession was sensationalized and not accurately portrayed. Many people who saw the movie including myself can still vividly recall the scene where a young Linda Blair (actress) spins her head 360 degrees and projectile vomits what looks like and has the consistency of pea soup at the priest. Never use a Hollywood movie as a reference guide for understanding possession and the nature of demons.

In Mark 5, we see that demons can speak through the host

body. Luke 11 shows us that demons desire human bodies as a place where they can find rest. The "I will" statement by a demon in Luke 11:24 proves that evil isn't a concept of inherent good and evil as the secular world and some Christians claim, but an actual entity or spirit being with cognitive abilities. This is very critical to understand. Demons do exist and are real thinking beings and not just some cosmic force of evil!

Once an exorcism is performed and the person is healed, the show is far from over… it has actually just begun. These individuals are at intense risk of either demonic retaliation for being cast out, or for repossession. I know it is hard to understand but demonic separation leaves a void; it almost feels like someone cut off your right hand and there is something missing because of the "bond" or attachment that had been part of that person's thought processes for so long. You would think the person would be overjoyed, but that euphoria is short lived.

Depression is common and these individuals are at a higher risk for suicide because word travels fast on the demonic grapevine that an "occupied" house has been vacated. Multiple demons will draw near to check it out. They will definitely attempt to infiltrate the thoughts of this person. There is no logical reason as to why a demon would want a person to commit suicide as opposed to repossession which would benefit a demon. Pure evil defies logic and does what it wants because it thinks it can. It is imperative that the demonically free person immediately devote their life and every day to God, and fill their mind with godly things. Evil and goodness can't occupy the same space. Jesus explains and warns of the dangers of "business as usual" after being freed. These individuals must devote their life to God from that day of liberation forward, no exceptions!

Warning Signs of Possible Impending Eventual Possession:

Hearing voices or being compelled by strong compulsive feelings. Here the demon is exploring how much control and influence it has over a person by remote control. Will the individual "listen" and act upon the commands of the voices in his or her head? The demon is just like the deep ocean scientist who sends an unmanned remote controlled submarine to the ocean bottom to gather information on the ocean's floor.

- Insomnia and re–occurring nightmares. Demons are trying to deliberately wear you down physically. Sleep is the time when the body rejuvenates itself. Continued disruptions in the ability to sleep peacefully places a severe drain on reasoning capabilities. They are hoping to make you too tired and worn out to care about protecting your soul where you would trade your soul for one good night's sleep.

- Chronic fatigue and low energy levels. Demons are depleting your energy because their demand far exceeds the energy the human body can produce. When medical causes are ruled out, rule in spiritual ones.

- Smelling foul repulsive odors or sulfur indicates a demon is not only close by but trying to make contact with a human. It means that they have crossed over through a portal into our physical realm. Since they don't have physical bodies, what the person smells is their "essence" (spirit) manifesting in the physical world.

- Sudden onset of depression or intense erratic mood swings. Because the mind is coming into contact with pure unadulterated evil energy it causes severe disturbances in the electrical impulses generated by the brain that can't handle such foreign vibrations.

- Inappropriate angry outbursts with bizarre unfounded accusations and paranoia of "someone is out to get me". This leads to withdrawal from everyday living and isolation away from friends, family, and things that they once loved to do. The demon is trying to prevent any and all attempts of intervention by others.

- Physical changes in the body. Weight gain or loss, gastro–intestinal issues, headaches, asthma like symptoms, and unexplained joint pains. These are metabolic changes due to the inability to integrate spirit energy with human energy.

- Frequent minor accidents or mishaps. As the demonic energy begins to integrate with its host there is a learning curve if you will over how the demon has to move in sync with the human body. The mechanical movements of the body in the early stages will appear klutzy. Also there is a power struggle over which "mind" is in control of the physical body.

- Self-destructive behavior including inflicting self-injury. Demons are like locusts. They will consume and destroy their host and then seek out another. Getting the host to perform acts of self-mutilation gives the demon a smug sense of satisfaction that *they* are the ones in complete control of the body.

If you or someone you know is experiencing any of the above symptoms it doesn't mean that they are about to be possessed. Rule out all medical and psychological causes first. Rule in direct involvement with bargaining or summoning a demon, Satanism, or other practices where the person grants permission for spirits to enter their body. Then and only then it requires more than just one of the above symptoms to suspect a potential demonic hostile takeover. What it does indicate is that a demon is in close proximity to that person attempting to breach their defenses and wear them down mentally, emotionally, and physically for the sole purpose of that soul's ruin either through self-destruction or possible possession. If however you or someone you know are experiencing any of these symptoms, and have willingly offered your body to be used as a conduit for spirit communications, be very worried. Seek spiritual counseling from a priest who understands spiritual warfare! Upper level demons who have been summoned by someone deeply involved in the occult want nothing more than to be able to possess that person. They can't of course unless you give them permission to do so. Despite the born again Christians who claim with full authority that a born again "believer" can never be possessed by a demon, that is simply not true. Free will dictates that you always have a choice to choose evil or good in everything you do regardless of your religious position. Demons will however attempt to torment, badger, and wear down the individual into willingly handing over their body and or soul to them.

Sleep Paralysis or Demonic Wrestling?

Many people who are tormented by demonic activity claim that they will awaken in the middle of the night to feelings of being strangled, or having some "thing" sitting on their chest making breathing almost impossible. Most times there is a feeling of being held down and physically unable move a muscle. Medical science tries to explain it as a simple case of your brain actually waking up before your body does, hence the mind and body disconnect. The medical term they use for this phenomenon is called, "sleep paralysis". Honestly that makes no sense seeing that the brain is in control of voluntary body movements and you have to think the thought (move my arm) before the body can respond (arm moves). In cases of demonic haunting, it IS a demon behind this disturbing night paralysis. They do this when you are the most vulnerable and not fully awake purposely so that you feel like you are wrestling with them alone. It is an act of intimidation to convince you that you are powerless over them.

There are strategies one can utilize to make demonic harassment go away. However, it requires following a comprehensive protocol and not just picking one strategy here and one there. Most times when demonic infestation has occurred, the demon has unpacked its bags and has no plans of leaving. It will become a battle of attrition, but one you **can** win if you follow through with the strategies and holy weapons I will outline in chapter ten. Miracles do happen! I encourage you to read about St. Bartolo Longo. He was a Satanist who became a Saint.

It is never too late to ask God to forgive you and heal you. When God hears your prayers and you feel he isn't answering, He isn't debating whether or not to answer that prayer. He is in the middle of orchestrating events in your life to help with what it is you have asked for. I know that for those of you suffering with demonic activity it seems like God has abandoned you but, trust me, he hasn't. As my dear friend Sister Francanne once said to me, "He is just behind the shadows".

"Who shall separate us from the love of Jesus Christ?...
For I am convinced that neither death nor life, neither

angels or **demons**, neither the present nor the future, nor any powers, neither height nor depth, nor anything else in creation, will be able to separate us from the love of God that is in Christ Jesus our Lord." Romans 8:35 and 37–39 (NIV).

Chapter 10

How to Protect Yourself From Evil

The best way to combat evil is to "fight fire with fire". From this day forward you can stop being a helpless victim of demonic influences and thought tampering by fighting the fire of hell with the fire of the Holy Spirit. It doesn't matter if you are or aren't plagued by direct demonic harassment; the strategies to combat demonic forces are the same. Following the guidelines outlined in this book and in this chapter will dramatically hinder the demon's ability to wreck havoc in your life. Never forget that Our Lady is the Queen of Angels and will someday crush the head of Satan, so ask for her help and intercession when you feel under attack by the evil ones. But before you can fully implement strategies designed to protect you from evil, you must adopt two pre–requisites of Christian living that keep demons off balance. They are acceptance and forgiveness.

Acceptance:
Changing Our Outlook and Taking Back Control

Without exception, trials occur to everyone in this world. Many times they blindside us, leaving us wondering what we did to deserve such punishment. Sometimes we are forced to choose between something awful and something even worse. Every trial has two sides: good and bad, and how we react to the trial is part of the trial itself. Trials are teaching moments no matter what course of action you choose to follow. Force yourself if you must to see the overall "big" picture for your soul and look for the lesson behind the trial. My late dear friend Will used to always remind me that "there is a lesson in everything" whenever I was hit by some unfortunate circumstance. It was an expression I didn't care to hear but now, years later, I realize the importance of those words. Never forget that you are never alone in these trials; God is only a prayer away and your guardian angel is forever in this life by your side!

Trials allow us to look at and examine parts of our lives we normally wouldn't focus on. Areas of our life that remain buried and hidden are brought to the light through struggles that test our character. Trials are designed to build character. Trials *are* a spiritual experience which will either draw you closer to God or to Satan, period! Grumbling, complaining, and demanding an answer from God only ingratiates you with the devil. He wants nothing more than to alienate you away from God by having you blame Him for your misfortunes. Acceptance however, takes that opportunity away from the devil to get you to turn your anger against God. The harder it is to embrace the positive learning side of a trial, the more we learn hope, patience, perseverance, and faith. Hope is future orientated, and despair (the opposite of hope) only traps us in the past and present. Demons attempt to manipulate trying situations to keep you feeling like a helpless victim of circumstance who has been abandoned or punished by God.

People tend to forget that this life is only transitional for eternal life. We are here to learn the mind of God and perfect our character as an heir to God's kingdom. Demons will attempt to convince you that trials are always a punishment from God which they are not! Accept trials as part of perfecting our soul and building of Godly character for our heavenly reward someday. Once we come out of the trial and we understand the lesson to be learned, we become beacons of light and hope to show others how to react correctly in similar situations. By being grateful for these unpleasant experiences we not only become aware of God's overall plan for our life but we are less selfish. James 1:4 (RKJ) states, "But let patience have her perfect work, that you may be perfect and complete, wanting nothing."

Forgiveness Disarms the Devil

By far, holding a grudge or being angry at someone else is the fastest, surest way to attract and keep demons in your space. Resentment is a powerful weapon that demons will use to snare you into even more negative thoughts and actions. Resentment and anger most often occur because we have been hurt either intentionally or unintentionally. Trust to some degree was broken leaving us vulnerable to disappointment. Staying angry or resentful seems to be self-justified because we take on the "power" to punish the wrongdoer. We stay angry or resentful to "teach them a lesson", but the reality is that the one we hurt the most is our self. We fear getting hurt again so it is easier to stay angry. Fear limits us but love sets us free. Forgiveness is the greatest gift we can give to others and in turn to ourselves.

Forgiveness on our part is a requirement if we want to be forgiven by God. Matthew 6:14–15 (RKJ) states very clearly this requirement: "For if you forgive men their trespasses, your heavenly Father will also forgive you. But if you forgive not men their trespasses, neither will your Father forgive your trespasses."

The evil ones don't want you to know this requirement so they go out of their way to infuse the situation with all sorts of negative energy deliberately to keep you from understanding a completely foreign and incomprehensible concept to them: mercy! Mercy is a powerful example of Godly love. God's mercy is endless. As children of God we are extensions of Him and therefore very capable of mercy and forgiveness ourselves. Don't let the evil ones convince you of the lie, "that is unforgiveable". Forgiveness is a choice to choose a godly approach to a demonically induced negative action. Leave the punishment up to God in His time and focus instead on praying for the wrongdoer to come to know Jesus and His mercy.

When you say to someone, "I will forgive you but not forget", in essence you haven't totally forgiven them completely but only partially. God isn't asking you to forget all the bad things that ever happened to you as if they never occurred, but He is asking you to not hold them over a remorseful person's head. Forgiving someone not only makes that person feel better, but we also feel better. Why? Besides it being a godly requirement, we feel better because the act of forgiveness is a "kill shot" to the heart of a demon. Forgiveness is such a powerful statement of agape (godly) love that demons who orchestrated the wrong doing against you cry out in torment. Forgiveness invites emotional and spiritual healing (godly love) crippling a demonic attack which is best visualized with this analogy: think of a demon who is pointing a gun at your face and threatening to shoot you. When you truly forgive someone, that infuriates the demon who pulls the trigger, but instead of a deadly bullet coming out, a bouquet of flowers (like the clowns use in a circus) pops out in your face instead. Who is the one that should be afraid now?

Bracing Yourself Against General Demonic Temptations

- Be sure to get a good night's sleep. Sleep deprivation causes mental exhaustion and confusion which lowers our ability to not only recognize demonic thought tampering, but to call out to heaven for help when faced with "ordinary" (every day) temptations or attacks.

- Take care of your body through good nutrition and exercise. Not feeling physically well is a big energy drain on both the body and mind. Being worn down is what the demons hope for as your defenses are weaker then. Don't make it easier for them to manipulate you by not taking care of your body.

- Stay away from places and people that just exude negativity as their negativity can be contagious if you expose yourself too long to it. Avoid questionable immoral activities as that is where there is sure to be a cluster of demons hanging out waiting to attach themselves to vulnerable people. Don't participate in conversations that are negative, angry, or depressing. From the minute you enter such a place demons will try to influence others to wear down your resolve to abstain from such activities. Negativity of any sort separates us from feeling God's presence in our life because God is pure love. Negativity is propagated by the demons deliberately to obscure our understanding of God's love for us. Ask yourself, "would Jesus be seen here?" If the answer is no then beat feet out of there.

- Spend some time with nature. Take a walk by the water or through some forests or fields. Observe the wildlife be it squirrels, birds, butterflies, or flowers. See and appreciate the beauty of nature and recognize the perfection of an awesome God who orchestrated such a beautiful creation. Focusing on appreciation crowds out any opportunity for demons to whisper a negative thought in your head. Appreciating the natural world also leaves us in amazement of God's power of creation and perfect balance in nature. Satan can't create; only destroy, so in nature we focus on creation and our Creator which proves that Satan is no match for our mighty God.

- Resign as the ruler of the universe and turn that position back over to God. Let go of self-criticism, judging others, and trying to control everything in your life and the lives of those around you. Becoming frustrated because things aren't going as you want them to only sets you up for negativity which is a great way that allows for demons to invade your space. You have no control over all the things that happen to you, but you do have total control on how you respond to them. Take all that wasted energy lost on trying to force life to fit into your perception of how it should be, and channel it instead on dealing positively with what life throws at you.

- Laugh at least a few times each day. Read a joke or funny story, watch a funny TV show, or remember a moment that makes you smile. Pure laughter is pure joy which is pure love. Laughter allows us a moment of reprieve from all the negativity we have going on in our life. Laughter is a glimpse of hope that reminds us that "this too shall pass". Laughter is healing.

- Pray every day and throughout the day. Prayer keeps us close to God. If you get close to God then the demons can't get close to you. Heartfelt prayers are like fingernails on a chalkboard to a demon. Pray for those who offend, hurt, or harm you. Don't hurl insults back or vow revenge no matter how unjustified the attack was against you. When we love God but stop short of loving other people it is because the evil ones have us only seeing their flaws and not their godly potential and value to God. Since God loves us despite our flaws, we too must love others despite their flaws. Praying for your enemy is a true sign of godly love. When we act out of love we are acting on the greatest power in the universe!! Just like God, our ability to love is limitless, so when we act out of love towards another (deserving or not) we are one with God in that moment!!! Pray the rosary and novenas as often as you can. Saying the rosary is a particularly powerful weapon against evil. There are many documented cases where praying the rosary actually changed the outcome of some dire circumstance.

- Be truthful in all things. Even the slightest deception done not to hurt someone's feelings, or to not make waves, is still deceit at its core. Deception invites demons. If someone gives you a "lucky charm" which you know is of occult origin and you accept that gift (because you didn't want to offend the person) with the full intention of throwing it away when no one is looking, that is deception. You falsely led that person to believe that you accepted and wanted that gift. You were being dishonest and no amount of justification will turn such behavior into a godly virtue. It is far better to be upfront and politely refuse the gift stating your conviction against such objects. Jesus himself said in John 8:31–32 (NIV), "If you hold to my teaching, you are really my disciples. Then you will know the truth, and the truth will set you free." Jesus told it like it was, never compromised, and never acted deceptively in any way. Demons can exploit dishonesty, but they can't manipulate honesty (truthfulness). The truth protects you from demonic attempts to capitalize on an act of dishonesty.

• Embrace, adopt, and practice godly love. Love is much more than just an emotion. It is the very essence of God. "Whoever does not love does not know God, because God is love." 1 John 4:8 (NIV). When we act out of love towards another, we are employing the greatest power in the universe! As children of God, just like our Father, our ability to act out of love is limitless. When we perform an act of unselfish love, we are close to and one with God in that moment because God is pure love! Staying close to God keeps us far away from Satan.

• Go to church regularly!! Going to Mass regularly places an invisible shield of protection around us. Partaking of the Eucharist (if you are a Catholic in good standing) is so vital in fortifying ourselves against all the snares of the devil. Matter of fact, the Eucharist is such a powerful weapon against the devil that I will elaborate on it under its own heading.

The Eucharist:
A Super Weapon Against Demons

Protestants flee in horror over the idea that the Eucharist is the actual body and blood of our Lord and Savior. While they will accuse us of not having a personal relationship with Jesus, partaking of the Eucharist brings us up close and personal with Jesus. Communion unites us most intimately with Jesus and increases sanctifying grace within us. In many Protestant churches, the minister with the dynamic speaking ability will not only draw in but captivate his audiences. Even within the same denomination, services are tailored by the minister of that particular congregation. People flock to the church that "grabs" their attention. In the Catholic Church however, it isn't the priest but the Eucharist that is the draw for its parishioners. The Mass centers on this very important focal point.

In Matthew 26:26–28 (RKJ), Jesus plainly institutes the Eucharist, "And as they were eating, Jesus took bread, and blessed it, and broke it, and gave it to his disciples, and said, 'Take, eat; this is my body.'

And he took the cup, gave thanks, and gave it to them, saying, 'drink you all of it; for this is my blood of the New Testament, which is shed for many for the remission of sins.'

Note that Jesus said, "This *is* my body" and not, "This represents my body".

Catholic priests at their ordination are given the authority and power by Jesus to change (known as transubstantiation) the bread and wine into the body and blood of Jesus during the consecration right before communion. The Eucharist is the body and blood Jesus shed for the remissions of all the sins of mankind including yours and mine. Paul in 1 Corinthians 10:16–17(RKJ) talks about how important Holy Communion is, "The cup of blessing which we bless, is it not the communion of the blood of Christ? The bread which we break, is it not the communion of the body of Christ? For we being many are one bread, and one body: for we are all partakers of that one bread".

I was told by a priest that right after receiving Holy Communion when we are one with Jesus, any prayer we offer is especially powerful. The Eucharist fortifies us against sinful temptations by strengthening our resolve to practice a virtuous life. More importantly, the Eucharist is an extremely strong and effective barrier of holiness against demonic temptations, manipulation, and harassment. The Eucharist is a demon's kryptonite which sends them running, screaming in horror. If you have no mortal sins hanging over your head and you are a practicing Catholic, receiving communion is a great preventative against demonic intrusions. It is a lot easier to prevent demons from gaining a foothold in your life than it is to rid them once they attach themselves to you. Drawing that close to Jesus so as to be one with him even if for just a short period of time, creates a hostile environment for demons where demonic cohabitation is not possible. Holiness and evil can't occupy the same space. The more often you take communion, the harder it will be to be influenced by demonic forces.

Confession:
Evicting the Devil From Your Life

I cannot stress enough how unconfessed sins are an open invitation for a demon(s) to come into your life. They are attracted to evil, and sin is evil in God's eyes. The sacrament of reconciliation (confession) offers God's mercy in the forgiveness of sins and the taking away of the guilt associated with that sin. It leaves us in a state of grace (until we sin again). You must confess your mortal sins before receiving the Eucharist, otherwise it is considered a sacrilege in our Lord's eyes. Mortal sins are the "big" sins which endanger our soul for eternal damnation. Committing a mortal sin means you have full knowledge of what you are doing is grievous to God, endangering your soul, and you don't care. In essence you are partaking of the buffet of evil set up at the devil's table, instead of at the table of our Lord. St. Paul is very clear about this; 1 Corinthians 10:21 (NIV), "You cannot drink the cup of the Lord and the cup of demons too; you cannot have a part in both the Lord's Table and the table of demons.

Telling a priest your sins also forces you to deal with them and not rationalize them away which is easy to do. Priests offer absolution from sins, and also can offer spiritual guidance on what you can do avoid repeating those sins. Telling someone else out loud your sins is very uncomfortable and humbling, but it forces us to think and act more responsibly. Don't be deceived into thinking that as long as you don't "commit" a sin, you are OK. Jesus made it very clear that just fantasizing about committing a sin in your head is just as good as acting it out; Matthew 5:27–28 (RKJ), "You have heard it said, Thou shall not commit adultery: But I say unto you, that whosoever looks on a woman to lust after her has committed adultery with her already in his heart."

The biggest deceiver we face isn't Satan himself, but ourselves. To a demon a sin is a sin, big or little, either one will give it a foothold in your life. Fantasizing about desiring something sinful means we no longer desire to follow God's will or direction. Focusing on mentally committing a sin means that eventually we will physically follow through with committing that sin. Confessing and talking out these impure thoughts helps bring clarity to how we want to live our life. It is best to choose one priest as your confessor. This way he gets to know you and can offer personal spiritual direction. In 1 John 1:8–10 (RKJ) we see the importance of confession, "If we say that we have no sin, we deceive ourselves, and the truth is not in us. If we confess our sins, he is faithful and just to forgive our sins, and to cleanse us from all unrighteousness. If we say that we have not sinned, we make him a liar, and his word is not in us."

Ten Strategies that Will Fortify Your Defenses Against the Evil Ones

1. Before even getting out of bed each morning consecrate the day to serving God. Say out loud that you are offering your free will to God to use to His benefit and for your personal edification. When faced with a temptation or even after falling and committing a sin, offer your free will to God again. This sends a message to the demons that you aren't going to make it easy for them the next time. Try reciting this prayer each morning, "Jesus through the Immaculate Heart of Mary, I offer you all my thoughts, words, and deeds of this day in union with the Holy Sacrifice of the Mass being offered throughout the world in reparation of my sins and the sins of the world, Amen." By consciously deciding to turn that day over to God, you are ready to put on the whole armor of God (Ephesians 5).

2. Remember that God is in charge and not the demons. Nothing happens without God's consent. Demons fear God even though they infest our reality as arrogant menacing presences that enjoy mocking God and all things divine. James 2:1(RKJ) makes this clear, "You believe that there is one God; you do well: the devils also believe, and tremble." Think of a demon as nothing more than a bully picking on someone he thinks he can frighten. Respond to demonic attacks as if you were responding to a two year old child throwing a tantrum. This puts you in charge of your emotions and not the demon. Fear

nourishes a demon and gives it power over you because when you are afraid you don't trust that God is in charge of your situation. Without fear the demons have no way of controlling you because by trusting in God you hold power over the demon. You are then emphatically stating that God's authority is no match for a demon.

3. Call upon your guardian angel regularly to stay by your side as a protector and to help keep you safe. They are with you 24/7. As soon as you sense danger of any sort, ask them to go in front of you to keep you safe. Ask them to guide you away from temptations, danger, and demonically engineered unwholesome activities. If you find yourself in situations where a person or persons are being demonically influenced to hurt you or someone else, ask St. Michael the archangel along with all the angels to come battle the demonic forces behind such an act.

4. Don't "wander and then wonder" what happened. Stay away from questionable and shady thoughts and activities. Trust me, if you tolerate a little evil, more evil is just around the corner waiting for you. Don't subject yourself to a questionable activity just to "fit in" and be a people pleaser. A relaxation of your morals is viewed as a weakness by the demon in charge of the activity and sends out a challenge to him to try to get you to commit sinful behavior. Stand up for God when faced with someone trying to coerce you into questionable activities. Don't be afraid to say "no", and defend righteousness. Saying nothing is agreeing with the devil. Walk away with your head held high. Satan places all sorts of distractions in our path deliberately to "stunt" our spiritual growth by having us focus on physical concerns. This shifts our focus away from communion with God and onto activities

that are only temporal and probably not conducive for spiritual growth. Heed Romans 14:22, "Happy is he who does not condemn himself in what he approves."

5. Keep your "eyes on the prize". This life is all about developing godly character and readying ourselves for eternal life with God. Shift your attention off from physical issues and focus on the spiritual. When you make a commitment to put God first in all you do, you will view life differently. You will no longer be a victim of circumstance. Petty trivial daily matters that used to feel so overwhelming no longer seem so important when put in context of the "overall picture". Physical principles and concerns that are replaced by spiritual principles will dramatically reinforce you against demonic assaults. Now you will be spending more time throughout the day reflecting on God, leaving very little "wiggle room" for demons to attempt to breach your mental fortress by getting you derailed onto worldly cares.

6. Don't be sucked into the vortex of negativity of others; it is infectious. Curb your tendency to be drawn into agreeing with such negative thoughts of others. Try to infuse something positive in attempt to redirect the focus of the person or persons who is negative. If that doesn't work then walk away from the negativity and focus on staying positive. If it is impossible to physically remove yourself from the situation then mentally walk away. Disengage from listening to the grumbling and think about something positive, make a mental list of all the good things that happened to you in the last day, month, or year. Sing a hymn or happy song in your head to block out the negativity of those around you.

7. Reflect on your thoughts and behavior periodically

throughout the day. Reflect on the good and not so good that you have done so far. This allows for more immediate course corrections if you are straying off the straight and narrow. It is a great way for us to "police" our thoughts, desires, and actions. It helps us refocus back onto our spiritual priorities and goals. Doing this also allows you to correct small mistakes before they become really big ones.

8. Develop a regular prayer life. All too often people pray only when they have a need. In a society bent on instant gratification, many will pray for five minutes and then give up because they don't see results. God didn't create us as beggars. God created us as His children and as such when we pray, we have to pray with a spirit of thanksgiving that God will answer our prayer. There is great disparity between what we think we need and what God knows we need, and Satan uses this to his advantage by convincing you that God isn't listening to you. Don't give up!! It takes time for God to orchestrate events in your life with His perfect timing. Prayers of praise and thanksgiving, and being thankful for the blessings God has bestowed upon you will make it incredibly hard for demons to gain a foothold in your life. Prayer is talking to God and He is always there to listen to you, be it beside you in the car, waiting in line at the checkout, or in church. Heartfelt prayer in your own words is something our Lord never tires of listening to.

Jesus is our model for prayer. He always said "thank you" to God prior to performing every miracle in the bible. He did this deliberately and out loud to show us that we need to incorporate gratitude (a spirit of thankfulness) in every prayer. When we develop the mind of Christ, then the answer to our prayer "seems" or "feels" right even if it wasn't exactly what we prayed for. By reflecting on God's blessings and being grateful for everything, we *will* feel worthy of God's love. That will help in rebuilding low self-esteem.

Pray earnestly and actually "feel" grateful for all your blessings... don't offer up lip service as God isn't fooled! After all, when you look into the face of God, do you want to see a friend or stranger?

9. Pursue a virtuous life. Practice the seven heavenly virtues of: prudence, justice, restraint, courage, faith, hope, and charity. By doing this you thwart the seven deadly sins or vices that demons use (wrath, greed, sloth, pride, lust, envy, and gluttony) to establish a hold over you. Trust in God's promises for you. We depend on God's grace for eternal life. Obedience to God's laws isn't an option but a requirement!

Practice acts of mercy (charity) at every chance without reservation or judgment. Whenever I run into a homeless person who asks me for spare change, I give it to them without thought. On occasion I have been with "devout" Catholics when this occurred who chastised me for giving money to someone who would obviously squander it on booze or drugs. They failed to realize what a golden opportunity it was for me to practice a heavenly virtue. It was a "pop quiz" from God to test my growth in the virtue of charity. I was asked to fill a physical need which I did. I was not asked to appoint myself as guardian over how this person would spend the money I gave freely. I am only being "judged" by God on my ability to give. The homeless person will be judged by God for how he or she utilizes this act of charity. It is not my place to pronounce judgment based solely on speculation. Jesus quotes Hosea in Matthew 9:13 (NIV) when he says, "But go and learn what it means: 'I desire mercy, not sacrifice'. For I have not come to call the righteous, but sinners." Besides we never know if the stranger who asks for an act of mercy might in fact be an angel. Hebrews 13:2(NIV) mentions this very fact, "Do not forget to entertain strangers, for by so doing some people have entertained angels without knowing it." Sometimes the small act of charity you do might just be the miracle the person was praying for.

10. Acknowledge demonic attacks. When an aberrant negative thought pops in your head, just say, "This is not my thought." When you find yourself in a situation that could lure you into sinning say, "This is a demonic trap that I must avoid". When you are around negative people and you feel that negativity creep into your soul say, "This negativity is rubbing off onto me from the other person and I won't accept it". By acknowledging that you are being influenced by an outside source, you take away some of the power of the demon orchestrating these things. Remember I said in chapter six that demons don't want you to believe they exist because this way they can do their dirty work in your life without obstruction. Demons will try to make you miserable and get you to blame yourself for those feelings and actions. By acknowledging you are under a spiritual attack when it occurs, not only have you exposed the demon but you can call on heaven to help battle whatever it is you're wrestling with.

When you narrowly escape a close call that could either seriously injure or kill you, don't say you got "lucky". Acknowledge that a demon tried to do harm to you but God wouldn't allow it so he ordered your guardian angel to thwart the attempt. Demons are trying to keep you ignorant of the spiritual war they are waging against us. If you begin to realize certain thoughts or actions are demonically induced, you will no longer leave freak accidents or occurrences up to "coincidence". The demons are trying to pull the wool over your eyes so you can't see what they are up to. Once you make the connection of acknowledging demonic attacks and that there is a spiritual battle for your soul, your eyes will be opened. No longer can a demon fool or trick you into feeling powerless over your weaknesses, or get you into a spirit of self-condemnation.

Effective Weapons to Use in Combat with Demons

Daily Devotional Readings

Daily devotionals and or reading biblical passages keep our mind centered on Godly principles. It encourages us to embrace a virtuous life in preparation for eternal life. Like it or not, when we die, we are going somewhere. What you do in this life will determine where you will be in the next. In a world that is dominated by Satan, daily devotional readings and reflections help us to not lose focus on why we are here. The more time you spend in reflection of godly principles, the less space in your head is available for demonic infiltration. Try to at least read one biblical passage a day and spend time reflecting on that passage when you are driving, waiting in line, etc.

Blessed Objects

Blessed objects such as medals, rosaries, scapulars, crucifixes, are known as sacramentals and are particularly effective in warding off evil. It isn't the object itself but the blessing performed by a priest that gives it the power to fight off evil. I recommend that a blessed crucifix hang above the bed in each room that someone is sleeping in, and above the main entrance into the house. It sends a strong signal that you are fortifying your living quarters with the power of Jesus, not only to the spirit world, but to humans who enter. I have found that my guests when they see crucifixes and holy prints all throughout my house tend to monitor their language. Even visiting non practicing Christians or agnostics upon seeing all the religious icons in my home will refrain from crude or off color remarks and conversations. In a sense I have consecrated my house to the Lord and it is quite clear to all who enter that I am a devout practicing Catholic who is serious about her faith. Sometimes my guests will ask why there is a religious motif to the house and that becomes a great opening to bring up the concept of spiritual warfare to them.

It is also advisable to wear either a blessed crucifix and or blessed medal of St. Michael the Archangel, Our Lady, a four way medal, or your patron Saint. Consider such items as a "mark" that you are a determined Christian. Wearing or carrying blessed objects offers some protection against the evil influences out there. It serves as a visual reminder to you to conduct yourself in such a way so as to bring honor to God and all things heavenly. The most offense sight to me is when I see music super stars wearing huge pectoral crosses and then behaving like children of the devil. That reeks of blasphemy. Wearing holy objects should be done with reverence. Jesus suffered terrible agony for your sins. Don't treat crucifixes and heavenly objects as jewelry because that is disrespectful to the great suffering and sacrifice He made for you.

Saint Benedict Medal

Saint Benedict medals are a crucial part of protecting yourself and property from demonic forces. Evil monks tried to poison Saint Benedict with poisoned wine and bread. When St. Benedict made the sign of the cross over the chalice, it shattered spilling all the tainted drink and a raven carried away the poisoned bread. This medal is designed to protect the wearer against evil influences of all sorts, witchcraft, temptations, and protection against storms and lightening. WEARING THIS MEDAL SHOULD BE DONE WITH REVERENCE AND FAITH. NEVER, EVER, IS THIS MEDAL TO BE CONSIDERED A "LUCKY CHARM" OR GOOD LUCK TALISMAN! A blessed medal of St. Benedict should be kept over the doors leading in and out of the home. Bury one at each corner of your property to protect your home. Keep one on you at all times whether you wear it or carry it in a wallet, pocket, car, or purse. The medal contains the initials of a prayer of exorcism against the devil. On the back side of the medal are the letters, CSSML that stand for the prayer, "CRUX SACRA SIT MIHI LUX! NUNQUAN DRACO SIT MIHI DUX!" (May the holy cross be my light! The dragon never my guide!). The medal has the letters, VRSNSMV–SMQLIVB and is the prayer of exorcism against Satan, " VADE RETRO SATANA NUNQUAM SUADE MIHI VANA! SUNCT MALA QUAE LIBAS. IPSE VENENA BIBAS." (Be gone Satan! Never tempt me with your vanities! What you offer me is evil. Drink the poison yourself!).

Prayer of Protection

At the first hint of trouble be sure to invoke the St. Michael prayer, and a prayer of protection against evil. Whenever I find myself in an environment that is full of negative energy, I invoke a prayer of protection from God that goes like this, "The light of God surrounds me, The love of God enfolds me, The power of God protects me." I also do this each morning upon getting out of bed because I just don't know who or what I will encounter for that day. As Christians we are all targets for Satan and his minions, who want nothing more than to destroy us by any means possible. We as flesh and blood cannot expect to be victorious against powerful intelligent spirit beings by ourselves. Asking for protection shows a spirit of humility, acknowledging that without God we are nothing and don't stand a chance against the assaults of fallen angels.

Holy Water and Blessed Salt

Holy water must be an essential part of your overall spiritual warfare plan. By far, holy water is the ultimate sacramental weapon that can kick some demon booty! Even non Catholics who use holy water properly will receive the same blessings and protections as that of a practicing Catholic. Holy water is like bug spray that repels demons. Decades ago it was common for Catholics to have a holy water font hanging by the main entrance of their home. As they would enter or leave the house, their fingers would dip into the bowl containing holy water and they would make the sign of the cross on themselves. Sadly today, this practice viewed as archaic has become almost extinct. This simple ritual done upon leaving the house offered a measure of protection from the evil influences that person would encounter in public. Performing the ritual when entering the home acted like a sanitizer, "disinfecting" them from any evil attachments they may have picked up while out and about. I strongly urge you do revive this practice.

Always carry holy water on your person and in your vehicle as a form of protection from evil. Before shaking hands with someone that gives me an uneasy feeling I rub a little holy water on my hands to ward off any evil influences. To be inconspicuous I carry my holy water on me in a small hand sanitizer bottle. Everyone just assumes it is hand sanitizer. If someone makes physical contact accidently or on purpose and I don't feel good about it, I will dab myself with holy water even after the fact. If I can make a sign of the cross on my forehead using holy water without being noticed, I do it. Otherwise it is just a simple rub. I have actually witnessed people that I sensed had an evil attachment recoil and back away after grabbing my hand to shake it, not knowing I put holy water on my hands. There are no toxic side effects from over use of holy water, so when in doubt, bring the holy water out!

Sprinkle some holy water in a room or make a sign of the cross with it over door jams to offer protection from evil, or to dispel any evil residual (or otherwise) that may be lingering in that area. You can do this with your vehicle too. Once blessed, there is no expiration date on how long the blessing is effective. All Catholic churches offer free holy water. Usually somewhere in the church itself is a large container of sorts with a spicket where you just bring your own bottle and fill it up yourself. Don't drain the holy water fonts found in the church doorways! If all else fails just ask the priest or his assistants for some. You can even bring your own container of water and have a priest bless it. Really there is no excuse for not having this essential weapon in your arsenal.

Blessed salt is extremely effective in warding off evil. It is an instrument of actual grace. Usually, a few grains are placed along window sills, and thresholds which prevents an evil spirit from passing over or through it. Sprinkle the entire perimeter of the outside of your house. Carry some in your car. After leaving someplace that you sensed was demonically charged, sprinkle a complete circle of salt around your car's perimeter before getting in. This prevents you from transporting a spiritual demonic hitch hiker. Place a few grains around your bed. As with all sacramentals, your faith is instrumental in whether the use of any adjuncts will be effective. Without belief nothing will work; with faith, all things are possible!

A Dire Warning!

I know there will be some readers who after finishing this book will want to storm the gates of hell, ready to ambush the enemy. Spiritual warfare isn't a crusade. There are casualties, and you yourself may become the biggest one. Don't deliberately seek out to banish evil. These supernatural forces of pure evil play dirty and are extremely cruel. They really don't like it when you "step on their turf" of the person they are tormenting or afflicting, and try to be someone's hero. If someone is under the influence of a demon and doesn't want to break free from that affliction, do NOT attempt to coerce, force, or badger them to see the error of their ways. This is asking their demon(s) to come after you. In my ministry I have had quite a few clients tormented by demonic spirits because they tried to do just that. Leave the "combat" for the Special Forces: people who are trained and have experience in dealing with these spiritual matters. Instead, the most effective weapon you can utilize that will be helpful for that person is prayer. Become a prayer warrior. Start a prayer group.

Also it is imperative that you respect a person's free will. Never use blessed salt or holy water in someone's home or business to rid their space of evil without their expressed consent first. If they don't want you to, then honor their wish no matter how badly you think you are helping them otherwise. To do so in secret is a form of deception which attracts the attention of the demon. God never forces His way on people so neither can you! People aren't always what they appear to be. It could be that the person invited evil into their life knowingly for whatever reason. If you use deception even with good intentions, it is still a violation of that person's free will and their demon WILL either attach itself to you or get one of his buddies to do so. You know the old saying, "The road to hell is paved with good intentions."

Be careful when using blessed salt. Use it correctly and fully. Don't just place salt on the front threshold to keep evil out and then not place salt on all the windows and entrances to a house. Demons aren't stupid, and not only will they enter through an unprotected entrance, but they will be very angry with you and all the occupants of the residence. Incorrect use of blessed salt conveys to the demon that you don't know how to fully protect yourself from them. You have now become a tasty morsel ready to be devoured by them.

Transference

Be extremely careful of "transference". This means that a demon attached to someone else gets attached to you. This can occur in various ways. Sometimes a person steeped in the black arts deliberately attempts to attach a demon to another person. This is accomplished by physical contact be it an "accidental" bump or touch. It is too complex to get into here, but go back to chapter six and read about energy exchanges. As soon as that happens, immediately dab yourself with holy water, call for heavenly help in prayer, and in Jesus' name demand that any demon attempting to attach itself to you, not do so. Do this silently without drawing any attention to yourself otherwise the fear you express is a gratifying sign to the initiator.

Transference can also occur when you get involved with someone who is battling a demonic infestation. By helping someone under these circumstances, if you aren't properly experienced, or have unconfessed sin(s), a demon will turn its wrath on to you for interfering. I have dealt with clients who attempted to help a friend plagued with demonic activity within their home. Having no understanding of just how devilish a demon can be, they ended up experiencing the exact same demonic activity after returning home.

Transference can also occur from cursed objects or trinkets. This is most commonly seen in the practice of voodoo, but black magic practioners also can cast a spell that attaches a demonic presence to an item. "Lucky charms", crystals, and pendulums are most frequently the objects deliberately infused with evil intent by vengeful individuals who hold a grudge against society, Christianity, or person or persons they don't like. Every now and then I come across these nefarious individuals selling their trinkets at flea markets or craft sales to unsuspecting buyers. Avoid lucky charms of any sort, and don't buy or accept an object from someone that you feel terribly uneasy about or around.

In Conclusion

This book isn't by any means a complete treatise on spiritual warfare and battling demons. I will be writing follow up books that go in more depth on this subject. This book's intent was for you to awake to the realization that demons are real and are working in your life. We are fast approaching the "end of days" and Satan knows his time as ruler of this world will come to an end. As a result he has ordered all under his command to intensify the war against you and me so that they (demons) can pervert and take with them as many souls as they can when cast into hell by an angel of the Lord on that great day.

"And I saw three unclean spirits like frogs come out of the mouth of the dragon, and out of the mouth of the beast, and out of the mouth of the false prophet. For they are the spirits of devils, working miracles, which go forth unto the kings of the earth and of the whole world. To gather them to the battle of that great day of God Almighty. Behold I come as a thief. Blessed is he that watches, and keeps his garments, lest he walk naked, and they see his shame." Rev. 16:13–15 (KJV).

No matter how bad things are in this life, Satan and his demons are outnumbered two to one by holy angels. I always say, "In the end we win!" Your personal struggle against demonic influences *will* be rewarded when Jesus returns and imprisons Satan and his fallen angels.

I want to leave you with the best news ever: "And I John saw the holy city, new Jerusalem, coming down from God out of heaven, prepared as a bride adorned for her husband. And I heard a great voice out of heaven saying, Behold, the tabernacle of God is with men, and he will dwell with them, and they shall be his people, and God himself shall be with them, and be their God. And God shall wipe away all tears from their eyes; and there shall be no more death, neither sorrow, nor crying, neither shall there be any more pain: for the former things are passed away. And he that sat upon the throne said, Behold, I make everything new. And he said unto me, write: for these words are true and faithful. And he said to me, It is done. I am the Alpha and Omega, the beginning and the end. I will give unto him who is thirsty the fountain of the water of life freely. **He that overcomes shall inherit all things; and I will be his God, and he shall be my son.**" Revelation 21:2–7 (KJV).

May God's love be with you always!